Athlone Fren

HENRI MIC

Athlone French Poets

General Editor EILEEN LE BRETON

This series is designed to provide students and general readers both with Monographs on important nineteenth- and twentieth-century French poets and Critical Editions of one or more representative works by these poets.

The Monographs aim at presenting the essential biographical facts while placing the poet in his social and intellectual context. They contain a detailed analysis of his poetical works and, where appropriate, a brief account of his other writings. His literary reputation is examined and his contribution to the development of French poetry is assessed, as is also his impact on other literatures. A selection of critical views and bibliography are appended.

The critical Editions contain a substantial introduction aimed at presenting each work against its historical background as well as studying its genre, structure, themes, style, etc. and highlighting its relevance for today. The text normally given is the complete text of the original edition. It is followed by full commentaries on the poems and annotation of the text, including variant readings when these are of real significance.

E. Le B.

Henri Michaux

by

PETER BROOME

UNIVERSITY OF LONDON
THE ATHLONE PRESS
1977

Published by
THE ATHLONE PRESS
UNIVERSITY OF LONDON
at 4 Gower Street, London WC1

Distributed by
Tiptree Book Services Ltd
Tiptree, Essex

U.S.A. and Canada
Humanities Press Inc
New Jersey

0 485 14605 3 *cloth*
0 485 12205 7 *paperback*

Printed in Great Britain by
The Garden City Press Limited
Letchworth, Hertfordshire
SG6 1JS

CONTENTS

NOTE

In references to Michaux's works throughout this study, the following abbreviations have been adopted:

Aill *Ailleurs*
BA *Un Barbare en Asie*
CG *Connaissance par les gouffres*
Ec *Ecuador*
ED *L'Espace du dedans*
EE *Epreuves, exorcismes*
ER *Emergences, résurgences*
FF *Façons d'endormi, façons d'éveillé*
FV *Face aux verrous*
GE *Les grandes épreuves de l'esprit*
IT *L'Infini turbulent*
LNR *La Nuit remue*
MM *Misérable Miracle*
Pl *Plume*
Q JF *Qui je fus*
VP *La Vie dans les plis*

Three important critical works containing previously unpublished material by Michaux are referred to as follows:
Bertelé René Bertelé, *Henri Michaux*, Seghers, 1965
Bréchon Robert Bréchon, *Michaux*, Gallimard, 1959
L'Herne *Cahiers de l'Herne*, No. 8: *Henri Michaux*, 1966

The cover portrait is a painting in watercolour and ink by Michaux dating from 1946–7. The author, general editor and publishers would like to thank Galerie Le Point Cardinal, Paris, and the private owner in Lyon for permission to reproduce it here.

I

BIOGRAPHY

There are enough warning-signs in Michaux's work to make any biographer uneasy. Not only has he always refused to entertain a facile relationship with his public, retreating behind the wall of the imagination and slipping from the grasp in bristling metamorphoses, but he has never felt any solidarity with his own life. In his early thirties he is speaking of a difference of tempo and a radical alienation:

> Tu t'en vas sans moi, ma vie.
> Tu roules,
> Et moi j'attends encore de faire un pas.
> ...
> Tu me désertes ainsi.
> Je ne t'ai jamais suivie.
> $\qquad$ (*LNR*, p. 92)

In his late forties he spits out his contemptuous refusal to be identified with anything which could be called *his* life, saying 'Je crache sur ma vie. Je m'en désolidarise' (*VP*, p. 9), just as in *Ecuador* (p. 88) he has rebelled against the possessive implications of a room specially prepared for him: 'Ma chambre! quelle histoire! me construire ma chambre!' He is a poet who does not inhabit his own life, and one wonders where one is likely to find the person who declares:

> Monsieur est absent
> Monsieur est toujours absent
> adieu je vous prie, il n'y a ici qu'empreintes.
> $\qquad$ (*QJF*, p. 65)

Who, indeed, is Michaux? Among the innumerable *qui-je-fus* who jostle for precedence in the author's dense inner space and among the faces, ill-formed and unreliable, which smear, splash or erode their way across his paintings, how does one compose an image of the real man? One must have doubts about which Michaux one has seen and to whom, if anyone, it corresponds. For he warns:

> Quand vous me verrez,
> Allez,
> Ce n'est pas moi
> (*LNR*, p. 177)

and, aware of the counterfeit nature of all identities, sets these words as the epigraph to one of his texts:

> Casanova dans son exil disait à qui voulait l'entendre: 'Je suis Casanova, le faux Casanova'.
> Ainsi de moi, Messieurs... (*LNR*, p. 187)

As he writes in *Ecuador* (p. 89):

> Peut-on être l'ami d'un traître!
> Ça c'est ma clef: Traître. Vous l'avez maintenant:

he will inevitably betray his own semblances and manifestations. As one attempts to stake a life around him, Michaux, one suspects, will always have slipped *ailleurs*.

Any biography must rely heavily on the *Quelques renseignements sur cinquante-neuf années d'existence* given by the poet to Robert Bréchon in 1958 (*Michaux*, Gallimard, 1959, pp. 15–23). But even here there is cause to be wary. For these skeletonic notes, written in the objective third person, form an 'alienated' autobiography. They are, as it were, a sloughed skin, offered somewhat ironically for general consumption. Moreover, the notations speed up to become increasingly perfunctory, like a hardly relevant shorthand, on reaching the period of adulthood. At that point they speak only of the barest external events, and one is left to hunt the real history, the evasive and complex inner life, in the poet's effervescent literary and graphic work which is its only authentic voice. Michaux has warned against pretending to reconstruct 'lives' on the wrong evidence:

> Quand je songe qu'il y a deux ou trois ânes qui se sont imaginés avoir reconstitué la vie de Rimbaud d'après sa correspondance!
> Comme si des lettres à sa sœur, à sa mère, à un pion, à un copain livraient quoi que ce soit. (*Ec*, p. 52)

Valuable as the Bréchon notes are, one should remember that they are, in a sense, the author's 'correspondance', a public communication in a comparatively superficial language.

Michaux was born in Namur, Belgium on 24 May 1899. He is not the first French poet to have felt the depressive influence of that country. Baudelaire summed up the spirit of Brussels as 'Laideur et Misère', incompatible with spiritual aspiration, and flinched from its 'Atmosphère hostile' where he saw 'Le regard et le visage de l'ennemi, partout, partout'.[1] Rimbaud was a caustic satirist of its bourgeois mediocrity and claustrophobic atmosphere, which fed his revolt and fired the energies of his inner vision. Michaux's own descriptions suggest a constricted environment without possibility or dimension, a corner of the globe transfused by only the most parsimonious vein of life:

Et cette campagne flamande d'hier! on ne peut la regarder sans douter de tout. Ces maisons basses qui n'ont pas osé un étage vers le ciel, puis tout à coup file en l'air un haut clocher d'église, comme s'il n'y avait que ça en l'homme qui pût monter, qui ait sa chance en hauteur. (*Ec*, pp. 12–13)

He speaks of his susceptibility to the cold and wind, 'le froid et le vent du nord qui est dur et souverain dans ce pays parfaitement plat où il passe comme un rasoir' (*Pl*, p. 109), his hatred of the vegetation with its 'branches qui n'offrent aucune ouverture' (*Ec*, pp. 62–3), impressions building to the conclusion: 'Il me hait le Nord, il me martyrise' (*Ec*, p. 178). Already there is a first taste here of the 'puissances environnantes du monde hostile' (*EE*, p. 9) against which Michaux's work is to prove such a versatile counter-measure.

His childhood was extraordinarily solitary, recoiled and unco-operative: 'Dès l'âge de six mois, je n'étais que refus: je ne voulais rien manger, plus tard, je ne voulais pas parler...J'opposais à tout une fin de non-recevoir. Je serrais les dents devant la vie' (quoted in René Bertelé, *Henri Michaux*, Seghers, 1965, p. 27). The details given to Bréchon, describing the years in Brussels from 1900 to 1906, speak of the same instinctive refusal to make the necessary compromise with physical reality, and depict a nature against the grain not responding to the customary laws of adaptation, attached to a self-sufficient unity or uniformity, and stubbornly impervious to the restless agitations of the outside world which threaten to infiltrate and disperse it:

Indifférence.
Inappétence.
Résistance.

Inintéressé.

Il boude la vie, les jeux, les divertissements et la variation.
Le manger lui répugne.
Les odeurs, les contacts.
Sa moelle ne fait pas de sang.
Son sang n'est pas fou d'oxygène.

Anémie.

Rêves, sans images, sans mots, immobile.
Il rêve à la permanence,
à une perpétuité sans changement.
Sa façon d'exister en marge, sa nature de gréviste fait peur ou
exaspère.
On l'envoie à la campagne. (op. cit., pp. 15–16)

A semi-autobiographical piece entitled 'Le Portrait de A.'
(*Pl*, pp. 107–17), a fictionalized portrait of himself in the vein of
Rimbaud's 'Les Poètes de sept ans', corroborates this picture of a
bleak, unremitting resistance to reality at large and a dogged
allegiance to some obscure spiritual identity:

Jusqu'au seuil de l'adolescence il formait une boule hermétique et
suffisante, un univers dense et personnel et trouble où n'entrait rien, ni
parents, ni affections, ni aucun objet, ni leur image, ni leur existence, à
moins qu'on ne s'en servît avec violence contre lui. En effet on le
détestait, on disait qu'il ne serait jamais homme.

Il était sans doute destiné à la sainteté. Son état était des plus rares
déjà. Il se soutenait comme on dit avec rien, sans jamais faiblir, s'en
tenant à son minimum mince mais ferme, et sentant passer en lui de
grands trains d'une matière mystérieuse.

Mais les médecins à force de s'acharner contre lui par l'idée fixe qu'ils
ont de la nécessité de manger et des besoins naturels, l'ayant envoyé au
loin, dans la foule étrangère de petits gredins de paysans puants, réus-
sirent un peu à le vaincre. Sa parfaite boule s'anastomosa et même se
désagrégea sensiblement.

The years from 1906 to 1910 were spent at boarding-school at
the village of Putte-Grasheide in the Campine region of Northern
Belgium. One can only guess at what they meant in terms of
imprisonment, hostility and frustration: as a further stage in the
secret drama of 'Partages de l'homme' (*Q JF*, p. 25). In Michaux's
first major text, published in 1927, the memory lingers of boarders
awakened by the din of dormitory bells and forced to go through
the motions of the day's procedures while their essential spirit
wanders aimlessly elsewhere 'entre clefs et autres objets de fer'

and the boys themselves are only 'morceaux humains ne pouvant se reposer et ne sachant que faire' (*Q JF*, p. 33). The Bréchon notes indicate a cold, harsh period, secretive and introverted, marked not only by the most fundamental solitude and alienation from his context, but by a spontaneous disgust for the baseness of physical necessities and for the mediocrity and limitations of his own nature:

> Secret.
> Retranché.
> Honteux de ce qui l'entoure, de tout ce qui l'entoure, de tout ce qui depuis sa venue au monde l'a entouré, honteux de lui-même, de n'être que ce qu'il est, mépris aussi pour lui-même et pour tout ce qu'il connaît jusqu'à présent.
> Il continue à avoir le dégoût des aliments, les fourre enveloppés de papier dans ses poches et une fois dehors les enterre. (op. cit., p. 16)

This repugnance to food is the gross physical symbol of a deeper tendency, seen for instance in *Ecuador*, to draw into himself only what serves some obscure inner purpose and to spit out all else in contempt or disinterest: 'Une fois pour toutes, voici: Les hommes qui n'aident pas à mon perfectionnement: Zéro' (*Ec*, p. 103).

The wall of foreignness casts its shadow over all Michaux's early relationships, not least those with his parents. The word 'étranger' recurs obsessively. Not only is it 'la foule étrangère de petits gredins de paysans puants' at the school of Putte-Grasheide, but as he reveals to Bertelé (op. cit., p. 27), 'Plus je retourne vers mon enfance, plus forte je retrouve l'impression d'avoir été un étranger chez mes parents'. Hostile references to parents lie rankling in innumerable corners of his work. The mother, without assuming the proportions of Rimbaud's 'bouche d'ombre', appears as a source of words which act as salt to a snail: 'Mère m'a toujours prédit la plus grande pauvreté et nullité...J'ai été la honte de mes parents' (*LNR*, p. 126) or 'Il y a neuf ans, mère me dit: "Je préférerais que tu ne fusses pas né"' (*LNR*, p. 140). The father, real or mythical, is an impassive figure offering no communication. One reads in 'Le Portrait de A.' that 'Son père avait ceci pour idéal: se retirer. Jamais il n'eut rien d'offrant. Il était prudent, très prudent, d'humeur égale et triste' (*Pl*, p. 109). It is a short step from this demoralizing presence to the monstrous overlord of 'Mon Roi' (*LNR*, pp. 13–19) whom the poet vainly tries to degrade and disfigure; and it is no surprise to see Michaux casting himself as the unprofitable servant with regard to paternal authority, saying:

> Etant mauvais cultivateur je perdis mon père
> non, n'apportez pas de lumière
> donc je le perdis
>
> (*EE*, p. 12)

nor to find the occasional wistful urge for a communion and comprehension which were never his: 'J'aurais tant désiré avoir un père. J'entends comme une femme…qu'on cherche, qu'on choisit et si l'on trouve, c'est un émerveillement' (*Ec*, p. 51). So, he and his parents remained locked in their separate priorities, an alienation prompting the categorical advice:

> Ne mettez pas les parents dans votre jeu,
> Il n'y a pas de place pour eux.
>
> (*LNR*, p. 181)

A brief entry in the South American diary shows how their image, pursuing him as far as the Amazon forests, heightened the sense of personal discrepancy, encouraging him to fall back more and more on his own fictions: 'Encore une lettre que j'écris à mes parents. Quel besoin j'ai de me vanter à eux. C'est ma revanche. On a tant prédit au propre à rien' (*Ec*, pp. 68–9). But he adds: 'Mais en fait je n'écris pas ma lettre. Je ne leur écris jamais. Je me méfie'.

In all, Michaux's was a joyless, defensive childhood, racked between participation and resistance, presence and absence, already sensitive to an unrelenting tug-of-war between *moi* and *non-moi* and to the encroachment of inimical forces. When he speaks of those supreme 'ennemis sans visage; de la racine, de la véritable racine d'ennemis', adding: 'Après tout, ils dominèrent déjà toute mon enfance' (*LNR*, p. 106), one can readily understand why at the end of his long South American journey, as if purging something from his system, he concludes:

> Il me semble que j'ai pas mal pleurnichaillé durant ce voyage.
> C'était plus fort que moi; comme une dette envers mon enfance. Je me comprends (*Ec*, p. 179);

and why, throughout his work, he continues to unearth and

wrestle with all that throbs 'dans le nid convulsif de misérables souvenirs d'enfance' (*FV*, p. 169).

One can hardly over-stress the significance of that early retreat into a state of 'Rêves, sans images, sans mots, immobile' and into the nascent mysteries of his 'boule hermétique' or *espace du dedans*. The portrait of the semi-fictional character A. (Michaux will be prone to spawn such characters in his own image) is centred on the attraction of the 'boule', with its radically different tempo of experience: 'Une grande langueur, la boule. Une grande langueur, une grande lenteur; une rotation puissante' (*Pl*, p. 109). It is linked, not simply with the mystical detachment symbolized by the 'grosses lèvres de Bouddha fermées au pain et à la parole' (*Pl*, p. 110) as they reject all commerce with the trivial overtures of the world, but with a perfect self-nourishing ecceity, a quasi-divine wholeness and sufficiency:

Ses premières pensées furent sur la personne de Dieu.
Dieu est boule. Dieu est. (*Pl*, p. 110)

And A. acknowledges his attachment to the idea of a fall from grace as an explanation of the disintegration of his 'boule', the loss of perfection and the ensuing history of martyrdom and frustration: 'A: l'homme après la chute' (*Pl*, p. 111). The severed contact with Infinity is a recurrent theme. Michaux refers back to the child's natural facility to live in the unlimited, 'dans les ondes sans fin du démesuré…dans une sphérique sphérifiante impression globale qui n'avait pas de fin', seeing this state as a strange separate planet on which we have all lived and then, as adults, progressively abandoned in exchange for limits and compartments (*GE*, p. 147).

The poet's early dream of saintliness draws meaning from this context. He addresses himself as 'moi, qui autrefois avait pourtant tellement aspiré à la sainteté' (*LNR*, p. 142) and reveals to Bertelé (op. cit., p. 30): 'Mais j'étais trop impressionné par les saints pour prendre les autres hommes et leurs écrits au sérieux'. This prestige extends far into Michaux's work. During the 1927 journey, he tells how the sight of simple mud houses always affected him, 'comme si des saints y habitaient' (*Ec*, p. 41); recalls his schoolboy's affinity, not to official theologians or religious figures, but to

le curé d'Ars, blackboulé à tous examens et questions théologiques, ou

Saint Joseph de Cupertino surnommé l'âne, et Ruysbrock l'admirable
qui faisait tout de travers, qui ne comprirent point infiniment de détails,
mais l'essentiel jusqu'à la moelle (*Ec*, p. 78);

and proclaims his incompatibility with the Equatorial Indians
because of a missing dimension: 'Ces gens n'ont pas de saints'
(*Ec*, p. 103). In Asia, on the contrary, he warms to the Hindus,
saying: 'Il n'y a pas de race plus sensible à la sainteté' (*BA*,
p. 43), and notes that anyone seeking saintliness will end his days
in the Himalayas, for it is there that 'la montagne est dégagée de
la saleté, des sens, de la glu végétale, des odeurs' (*BA*, p. 106)—
words reminding one of his own initial revulsion to food, smells
and contacts.

During the years of schooling in Brussels from 1911 to 1914,
and then under the grey mental imprisonment of German occupation from 1914 to 1918, Michaux discovered the potential life-line
of words. As for the adolescent A., 'Dans l'ensemble, les livres
furent son expérience' (*Pl*, p. 112). The Bréchon notes describe a
somewhat wayward, directionless reading, in which the poet,
interrogating words like signs, seeks especially a contact with
those who have penetrated some secret of *surnature*, and calls on
language to burst the mould of conformity and reality and plunge
into untried extravagances:

> Lectures en tous sens. Lectures de recherche pour découvrir les siens,
> épars dans le monde, ses vrais parents, pas tout à fait parents non plus
> cependant, pour découvrir ceux qui peut-être 'savent' (Hello, Ruysbrœck,
> Tolstoï, Dostoïevsky). Lectures des *Vies* des saints, des plus surprenants,
> des plus éloignés de l'homme moyen. Lectures aussi des excentriques, des
> extravagants ou des 'Jeune Belgique' à la langue bizarre qu'il voudrait
> plus bizarre encore. (op. cit., pp. 17–18)

'Le Portrait de A.' proposes an unusual view of the 'divinity' or
infinity of literary language. Whereas material phenomena are a
mere crust or facade, hard and inexpressive, words touch a fluid
and levitational world beyond: 'Le livre est souple, il est dégagé.
Il n'est pas une croûte. Il émane. Le plus sale, le plus épais
émane. Il est pur. Il est d'âme. Il est divin' (*Pl*, p. 112). The
protagonist himself reads in a fitful, inattentive way, by-passing
words, meanings and intelligible content in order to commune
vaguely, telepathically, with some boundless and ill-determined
inner flux: 'Car tant que son fond restait indécis et mystérieux et

peu palpable, son attention consistait à trouver dans un livre ce même univers fuyant et sans contours'. Already one can sense here those rapid *parcours* beyond the fringe of language into the movements and impulses of an inner space which are to be the hallmark of Michaux's literary experience.

But more important than the books of others were Michaux's relationships with his own language. He chooses two memories in particular as the major events of the period of his early teens. The first was his 'Découverte du dictionnaire, des mots qui n'appartiennent pas encore à des phrases, pas encore à des phraseurs, des mots et en quantité, et dont on pourra se servir soi-même à sa façon' (Bréchon, p. 17): the discovery of words in a state of *disponibilité*, uncommitted and not slaves to the ready-made. The second was his learning of Latin, 'belle langue, qui le sépare des autres, le transplante: son premier départ' (Bréchon, p. 17). This is a premonition of language used, not as communication, but as self-protection against reality and the means of access to a private *ailleurs*. A few years later comes another discovery:

Première composition française. Un choc pour lui. Tout ce qu'il trouve en son imagination! Un choc même pour le professeur qui le pousse vers la littérature. Mais il se débarrasse de la tentation d'écrire, qui pourrait le détourner de l'essentiel. Quel essentiel? Le secret qu'il a depuis sa première enfance soupçonné d'exister quelque part et dont visiblement ceux de son entourage ne sont pas au courant. (Bréchon, p. 17)

The germ of the future writer lies here: in these untapped reserves of image or 'unreal' material eager to burst on to the page and demand existence, and in the dichotomy between two selves, one shocked and surprised by the unruly revelations of the other. But for the moment there is a continued resistance to words. In the case of the writings of others, 'Je lis très mal, repoussant incessamment, avec haine, refus et mauvaise foi' (*Ec*, p. 74). In the case of his own words, he cannot quite conquer the feeling that they are an inferior concession forced from him by reality, a breaking of faith with an inner communication which transcended words; nor can he easily reconcile them with those 'Rêves, sans images, *sans mots*' and the 'grosses lèvres de Bouddha fermées au pain et *à la parole*'.

After his *baccalauréat*, with the University closed because of the

Occupation, there followed two years of aimless, inconclusive
'bricolage intellectuel'. In 1919 he prepared medical entrance
examinations, but did not sit them and finally abandoned the
idea of medicine. He thought of joining the Benedictine order,
but his father refused permission. These were the culminating
years of a foundering, disorientated youth. 'A l'expiration de
mon enfance', he writes, 'je m'enlisai dans un marais' (*EE*,
p. 25). It was a period of *non-événement*, haunted by the problem of
action and involvement. For the character A., it is a kind of
pre-natal life: inside are all sorts of flexing muscles but these are
incapable of propelling him as a fully formed being into the
world. Michaux says: 'D'une façon plus globale, ma vie même,
ma vie active est partie tard. Je commence seulement maintenant
ce que d'autres entreprennent à vingt ans' (*FF*, p. 57) and:
'Dans ma jeunesse, plus tard encore, je suis resté persuadé qu'il
n'y aurait pas d'événement, que j'arriverais au bout de la vie
sans' (*MM*, p. 174). Yet the moment comes to break the self-
enclosed *boule*, together with vacuous dreams of perfection, and
establish oneself in and through reality. The history of A. is
revealing: 'Un jour, à vingt ans, lui vint une brusque illumination. Il se rendit compte, enfin, de son anti-vie, et qu'il fallait
essayer l'autre bout. Aller trouver la terre à domicile et prendre
son départ du modeste. Il partit' (*Pl*, p. 114).

In 1920, Michaux embarked from Boulogne on a five-mast
schooner. In the same year, he signed up again on a ten thousand
ton collier, *Le Victorieux*, leaving Rotterdam for North and
South America, with ports of call at Savannah, Norfolk, New-
port News, Rio de Janeiro and Buenos Aires. He speaks of a
'Camaraderie étonnante, inattendue, fortifiante' (Bréchon, p.
18) with his fellow crew-members, as if savouring an interlude of
unprecedented adhesion in this preliminary floating *ailleurs*,
with its somewhat transient and unreal community. On returning to Rio, the crew protested against bad conditions on board,
and in solidarity with the others he walked out on what he calls
'le beau navire'. In 1921, he was back again in Marseilles. His
own descriptions sum up the sense of relapse, fruitlessness and
frustration:

Le désarmement mondial des bateaux (ex-transports de troupes et de
vivres) est à son maximum. Impossible de trouver un engagement. La
grande fenêtre se referme. Il doit se détourner de la mer.

Retour à la ville et aux gens détestés.
Dégoût.
Désespoir.
Métiers et emplois divers, médiocres et médiocrement exercés.
Sommet de la courbe du 'raté'. (Bréchon, p. 19)

No less than for Rimbaud, whose 'Les Poètes de sept ans' depicts him on the threshold of some essential marine experience, 'pressentant violemment la voile', or Baudelaire, whose rhythms conjure up subtle symbolic *correspondances* between the ocean and the deeper oceanic movements of the human spirit, the sea holds a supreme significance for Michaux. He writes,

Tournant le dos, je partis, je ne dis rien, j'avais la mer en moi, la mer éternellement autour de moi.
Quelle mer? Voilà ce que je serais bien empêché de préciser.
(*EE.* p. 121)

The first definition of the life of A. is 'une de ces vies insignifiantes, et pourtant Océan, Océan' (*Pl*, p. 107). *Qui je fus* (1927) contains this buoyant lyrical response:

Pour moi je retourne à l'eau de l'océan. Adieu
J'ai entendu le clacquerin des paquebots, j'embarque...
Par très mauvais temps je m'agrippe au grand pelé, l'oreille contre, ça fait toutes sortes de bruits; entre deux rafales je regarde venir les houlons crêtés de sabrouse
et parfois cette grosse eau se fait si calme et comme agonisante, on se sent profondément heureux. (p. 78)

On the other hand, the retrospective 'Portrait de A.' gives a very different picture of the period of his life at sea, one of waste, superfluity and pain: 'Pauvre A., que fais-tu en Amérique? Des mois passent; souffrir; souffrir. Que fais-tu à bord de ce bateau? Des mois passent; souffrir, souffrir. Matelot, que fais-tu? des mois passent, souffrir, souffrir' (*Pl*, p. 115). And the decision to set off leads only to personal conflict: 'Ce n'était pas orienter sa vie, c'était la déchirer'. Moreover, his next Atlantic crossing in the *Boskoop* in 1927 works no miracles: '*Boskoop*! grand aveugle qui traverse l'Atlantique. On serait dans un sac, ce serait pareil' (*Ec*, p. 17).

1922 was a crucial year of exploratory probings into the possibilities of literature. Michaux felt the shock of Lautréamont: 'Lecture de *Maldoror*. Sursaut...qui bientôt déclenche en

lui le besoin, longtemps oublié, d'écrire' (Bréchon, p. 19). Elsewhere he acknowledges those 'copains de génie que j'ai tant
aimés, Ruysbrœk et toi Lautréamont' (*LNR*, p. 186). One can
appreciate the influence of the Montevideo poet: his clenched
revolt, his multiple defensive fronts against the world, the bristling energies of his mental substrata, the powers of imagination
used as an instrument of metamorphosis and private salvation.
It was also the year of Michaux's own first publications in the
Brussels review *Le Disque vert* directed by Franz Hellens, one of
the few to see the originality and promise of the young man.
Even so, the final step into a world of words incompatible with a
more essential communication and into the conventional rôle of
writer proved almost impossible to make:

> Toujours réticent. Il n'aimerait pas 'devoir' écrire.
> Ça empêche de rêver. Ça le fait sortir. Il préfère rester lové. (Bréchon,
> p. 19)

He describes the same conflict of feeling in 1924, by which time
he had left Belgium for good and settled, however insecurely, in
the artistic atmosphere of Paris:

> Il écrit, mais toujours partagé.
> N'arrive pas à trouver un pseudonyme qui l'englobe, lui, ses ten-
> dances et ses virtualités.
> Il continue à signer de son nom vulgaire, qu'il déteste, dont il a honte,
> pareil à une étiquette qui porterait la mention 'qualité inférieure'. Peut-
> être le garde-t-il par fidélité au mécontentement et à l'insatisfaction.
> (Bréchon, pp. 19–20)

Just as a few years earlier in the doldrums of those 'emplois
divers, médiocres', Michaux as a teacher at a small provincial
school in Dinant near Namur could only feel the discrepancy and
emptiness of his rôle, saying 'A. est nommé professeur! Sottise!
L'Océan est au-dessous; se cache, se défend par les armes propres
à l'Océan, qui sont couche sur couche et enveloppements' (*Pl*,
p. 117), so he cannot adopt the finitude of the literary label.
Writing, like his name, is a meagre, derisory materialization of a
sea of possibilities and latent voices, and he will always be chafed
by the urge to be somewhere else and someone else, someone
more than the travesty which has to congeal itself in the name
'Henri Michaux'.

His first years in Paris were largely solitary, miserable and impoverished. He has already referred to the closing of a vital window and the claustrophobic return to the city and its hated populace. In *Ecuador* (p. 83) he writes: 'Pour une ville, un esprit d'une certaine dimension ne peut avoir que haine. Rien n'est plus désespérant'. Paris he sums up emptily as a 'grand bordel où l'on parle français' (*Ec*, p. 178), and there is no mistaking the bitter tone of these words written in 1928, 'Argent! argent, je parlerai un jour de toi...A perte de vue en arrière ma vie est dans ce carcan' (*Ec*, pp. 88–9). One should add to this picture the ever-present ghost of insomnia and physical illness: in particular a cardiac deficiency and its accompanying anxieties, which lurk in such remarks as: 'S'il y a un Karma et une expiation naturelle dans une vie suivante, le legs d'un cœur défectueux serait parmi les "legs les plus vengeurs, les plus expiateurs" ' (*Pass*, pp. 13–14). These were, however, the years of influential contacts in the world of literature and an increasing tempo of literary creation of his own: pieces in *La Revue européenne*, *Les Cahiers du Sud*, *Commerce*; a meeting with Jean Paulhan of the *Nouvelle Revue Française* who was to be instrumental in the publication, in 1927, of *Qui je fus*; and above all the beginning of a life-long friendship with Jules Supervielle who gave him a hitherto unknown warmth of encouragement and understanding. Michaux has spoken to Bertelé of this meeting of minds as the 'révélation de la poésie vivante', saying: 'Je voyais enfin un homme formé et transformé en poète, un homme que la poésie habitait comme je croyais jusque-là que seule la musique le pouvait' (op. cit., p. 32). This was also the period of the Surrealist revolution, with its aggressive illogicality, its twisting of the starched neck of language, its imaginative inventions, its wells bored into the subconscious, its dream-accounts and automatic writing. But Michaux, hostile to systems and literary theories, collective movements and exhibitionism, developed in the margin in his own original fashion. He had no need to become part of the external *brouhaha* of Dada to appreciate mental disorder and heterogeneous creation: 'L'esprit, naturellement, est dadaïste. Une minute dans un cerveau, c'est des tables, des rayons de soleils, des chiffres, des fleuves, des losanges, des mélodies, des bruits, du rouge' (*Q JF*, p. 16); nor, though he shared their aim, did he need the rapidly predictable tricks of the trade of the Surrealists: 'le merveilleux surréaliste est monotone, mais entre

le merveilleux et quoi que ce soit, je n'hésite pas. Vive le merveilleux!' (*Le Disque vert*, 1925, No. 1, p. 86). The names to
flash across his screen in 1925 are not Breton, Soupault or Desnos,
but 'Klee puis Ernst, Chirico...Extrême surprise. Jusque-là, il
haïssait la peinture et le fait même de peindre, "comme s'il n'y
avait pas encore assez de réalité, de cette abominable réalité,
pensait-il. Encore vouloir la répéter, y revenir!"' (Bréchon,
p. 20). This discovery of painting, not as a representational art
mirroring reality, but as the direct translation of mental space,
taut with fantasy, anguish and humour, will be the essential
stimulus to Michaux's own explorations of this 'second language'
not many years later.

But the superficies of artistic Paris were no palliative to a poet
craving dimension and seeking untrodden routes into his deeper
self. Michaux is soon to become that restless *déraciné* who finds
his only semblance of salvation in perpetual *mouvements* and
parcours. In 1927, with the Ecuadorian poet Alfredo Gangotena,
he set off for a year to Quito and the Amazon. *Ecuador* (1929) is
the anti-lyrical log-book of the journey, a largely sterile encounter with a meaningless reality which did nothing to relieve his
'larves et fantômes fidèles' (*Ec*, p. 76). In the first weeks of 1929
he was back again in Paris, only to rebound, immediately after
the deaths of his father and mother within ten days of each
other, into a series of new, compulsive departures. It was as if he
had to demolish the myth of 'belonging':

Voyages en Turquie, Italie, Afrique du Nord...
Il voyage *contre*.
Pour expulser de lui sa patrie, ses attaches de toutes sortes et ce qui
s'est en lui et malgré lui attaché de culture grecque ou romaine ou
germanique ou d'habitudes belges.
Voyages d'expatriation. (Bréchon, pp. 20-1)

It was not until 1930-1, however, that the definitive break was
made with the habits of Europe and with the paralysing compartments of Western thought and behaviour:

Enfin *son* voyage.
Les Indes, le premier peuple qui, en bloc, paraisse réponde à
l'essentiel, qui dans l'essentiel cherche l'assouvissement, enfin un peuple
qui mérite d'être distingué des autres.
L'Indonésie, la Chine, pays sur lesquels il écrit trop vite, dans
l'excitation et la surprise émerveillé d'être touché à ce point, pays qu'il

lui faudra méditer et ruminer ensuite pendant des années. (Bréchon, p. 21)

Here, one sees Michaux excitedly sucking in a complexity of new culture which will feed his mental processes for years to come and provide the means for new resourceful relationships with reality and with himself.

At this point, one has already pushed well into Michaux's literary work (*Qui je fus, Ecuador, Mes Propriétés, Un certain Plume, Un Barbare en Asie, La Nuit remue*) and a deeper evidence is available with which to trace a life. It is appropriate to close the outer shell, allowing the creature its authentic inner movements, and to read the language of its strange secretions. One can only leave the same formal outlines as those left by the poet to Bréchon:

1932	Lisbonne-Paris.
1935	Montevideo, Buenos Aires.
1937	Commence à dessiner autrement que de loin en loin. Première exposition (Galerie Pierre à Paris).
1938–9, Meudon	S'occupe de la revue *Hermès*.
1939	Brésil (Minas Geræs et Etat de Rio).
1940, janvier	Retour à Paris. En juillet, l'exode. Saint-Antonin. Ensuite le Lavandou.
1941–2	Le Lavandou avec celle qui sera bientôt sa femme.
1943	Retour à Paris. Occupation allemande (la seconde).
1944	Mort de son frère.
1945	Affaiblie par les restrictions alimentaires, sa femme contracte la tuberculose. Ensemble à Cambo. Amélioration.
1947	Presque la guérison. Voyages de convalescence et d'oubli des maux en Egypte.
Février 1948	Mort de sa femme des suites d'atroces brûlures.
1951–52–53	Il écrit de moins en moins, il peint davantage.
1955	Naturalisé français.
1956	Première expérience de la mescaline.
1957	Expositions aux Etats-Unis, à Rome, à Londres. Se casse le coude droit. Ostéoporose. Main inutilisable. Découverte de l'homme gauche. Guérison.

Et maintenant?

Malgré tant d'efforts en tous sens, toute sa vie durant pour se modifier, ses os, sans s'occuper de lui, suivent aveuglément leur évolution familiale, raciale, nordique... (Bréchon, pp. 22–3)

One reads such jottings in the knowledge that they do scant justice to crucial moments of Michaux's life: the tormented, self-searching wanderlust which propelled the writer to-and-fro in the 1930s; the effervescence of mystical enquiry surrounding the review *Hermès*, with its key-figures Bernard Groëthuysen, André Rolland de Renéville and Mme. Mayrisch Saint-Hubert, of which Michaux was chief editor for two years; the tensions and stresses of Occupied France, evident in the poet's *Epreuves, exorcismes* (1945) where, without being specifically 'committed', he pursued his own private Resistance movement, struggled to salvage both his own identity and the essence of human spirituality from the jaws of chaos and void, and turned painfully to requestion his relationship with other men; the anguish of his wife's prolonged illness, so soon after their marriage, and the vicious irony of her death in a burning accident, so soon after her convalescence, an emotional trial recorded in the lyrical pages of *Nous deux encore* (1948), a sequence of fragile notes transmitted on a plaintive spiritual telegraph; the surprising post-war upsurge of his paintings, so disturbing and defiant, which left critics and fellow-painters searching for definitions, stranded between such inadequate labels as 'Surrealist', 'abstract' or *tachiste*, but which soon extended their obscure impulses from the left-bank galleries of Paris (Galerie Rive Gauche, Galerie René Drouin, Galerie du Dragon) to Seattle (1954), New York (1956), Rome (1956), London (1957), Venice (1960), Stockholm (1960) and eventually back to the walls of the Musée national d'Art moderne in Paris for the challenging retrospective of 1965; the pulverizing energies, the turbulent journeys of the mescalin revelation and the labyrinth of his experiments with hallucinogenic drugs from 1956 onwards; the apparent triviality of a mishap such as a broken arm, which became the trigger, as seen in his text *Bras cassé* (Fata morgana, 1973), for the exploration of a host of 'perceptions déroutantes', of a network of signals and silent desertions within the body; and now, in his late seventies just as in his late fifties, the persistent refusal of a man to submit to fatality, acceptance, determinism. 'Tu t'en vas sans moi, ma vie' (*LNR*, p. 92): most certainly, in the case of Michaux, the formal biography is but a passing shadow.

II

POETICS

No one has done more in this century than Michaux to bring poetry out of its indulgent self-contemplation and make it work for its living. What he says of the spirituality of the Hindu applies to himself and poetry: 'Dans l'ordre spirituel il veut du rendement. Il ne fait pas de cas de la beauté...Il ne fait pas de cas de la vérité comme telle mais de l'Efficacité' (*BA*, pp. 22–3). It is not a question of words fondling words and setting up a mutually flattering verbal world apart, but of words intervening dynamically in the heart of the problem of existence and judged solely on their practical success. For this reason Michaux speaks of his poetic means as weapons and tools: 'Mes moyens d'expression, c'est-à-dire mes armes, ces outils et signes de ma puissance, qui me donnent capacité d'intervention, d'expression, du moins la plus immédiate (dents de devant)' (*FF*, p. 144). The resultant poem is not an artistic product to be savoured according to the laws of some aesthetic harmony. It is, ideally, a sorcery or therapy, an act of personal salvation, however provisional, valuable for the transformation it can work either on reality or on the self: 'L'art qui sait être sorcier, ou guérisseur, ne peut-on en attendre cette réussite? Cette révélation?' (*Pass*, p. 187). Michaux never loses this desire to make words do something more than words, to intervene, metamorphose, revolutionize, recompose, as if the energy of poetry should stir and redistribute the molecules of reality or implant vision as fact. As he says in 'Portrait d'homme' (*Cahiers de l'Herne*, No. 8, p. 337),

Il serait bien écrivain, car il a de continuelles inventions mais il voudrait les voir, non écrites, mais réalisées, et que nos conditions d'existence changent du tout au tout, suivant elles. Il se gargarise peu de ses inventions, au rebours de l'écrivain, il veut voir l'impossible miracle, c'est-à-dire leur passage dans la vie. (C'est donc plutôt à la magie qu'il aspire.)

The same demiurgic fascination is apparent in his account of the traditions of Southern India. 'C'étaient des gens qui aimaient entre autres la magie des mots', he writes, adding '*Magie* dans le

sens fort du mot'; and he quotes the example of Tulsi Das, the
poet of the *Ramayana*, who meditated so intensely when in prison
that a host of monkeys invaded the town and brought about his
liberation: 'Bien, maintenant ouvrons un concours: Quel est le
poète européen qui en puisse faire autant?' (*BA*, p. 116). That
writing is an act for Michaux and not a juxtaposition of artistic
effects is apparent in the following description of the poetic
process:

> Il écrit...
> Le papier cesse d'être papier, petit à petit devient une longue, longue
> table sur laquelle vient, dirigée, il le sait, il le sent, il le pressent, la
> victime encore inconnue, la victime éloignée qui lui est dévolue.
>
> Il écrit...
> Son oreille fine, fine, son unique oreille écoute une onde qui s'en vient,
> fine, fine, et une onde suivante qui s'en va venir d'un lointain d'âge et
> d'espace pour diriger, amener la victime qui devra se laisser faire.
>
> Sa main s'apprête.
> Et lui? Lui, il regarde faire.
> Couteau depuis le haut du front jusqu'au fond de lui-même, il veille,
> prêt à intervenir, prêt à trancher, à décapiter ce qui n'est pas ne serait pas
> sien, à trancher dans le wagon que l'Univers débordant pousse vers lui,
> prêt à décapiter ce qui ne serait pas 'SA' victime...
> Il écrit... (*EE*, pp. 117-18)

Here, the paper is no longer that purified 'vide papier que la
blancheur défend' (Mallarmé, 'Brise marine') but a place of
blood and violence, an intimate battlefield where the relations
between the writer and the objective world, between 'bourreau'
and 'victime', are constantly reworked and turned into an
acceptable balance of power. Poetry becomes an operating table,
far more urgent and carnal than that admired by the Surrealists
on which a sewing machine and an umbrella are brought into
provocative confrontation, and the poet himself is transformed
into a living instrument, pulled by some unavoidable fate to
perform surgery on the matter of reality. Writing conjures up a
rhythm which connects with other rhythms to become an active
force and bring on the sacrificial moment. Contrary to the
impression given by a title such as *Ailleurs*, poetry for Michaux is
not an escapist practice, a literary retreat where the imagination
can embroider at will. It is a committed weapon closely attached
to his own flesh and to the heart of his torments and obsessions:

'Un écrivain est un homme qui sait garder le contact, qui reste joint à son trouble, à sa région vicieuse jamais apaisée' (*Pass*, p. 148). It is used in an infinity of strategies in order to 'tenir en échec les puissances environnantes du monde hostile' (*EE*, p. 9). It is a *Poésie pour pouvoir*: called on to reinforce, to repair, to deflect, to distort, to demolish, to contribute in innumerable ways to the temporary relief of the author's unappeasable *problème d'être*.

One of Michaux's most important statements on the nature of poetry is the Postface to *Mes Propriétés*. He stresses its therapeutic function, saying: 'Par hygiène, peut-être, j'ai écrit "mes propriétés", pour ma santé' (*LNR*, p. 203). For those who feel 'out of order' or ill-adjusted to reality, it elaborates figures, images, structures which correct a balance, safeguard a threatened equilibrium and nourish what was formerly in a state of deprivation. It is an art of compensation, creating possession where there were lacks, a substitute personality where there was an insecure nonentity, relief where there was tension. It is essentially a non-aesthetic poetry, governed not by artistic but by psychological needs, and improvised with whatever fortuitous fragments come to hand:

Ils font leur personnage selon leur force déclinante, sans construction, sans le relief et la mise en valeur, ordinaire dans les œuvres d'art, mais avec des morceaux, des pièces et des raccords de fortune où seule s'étale ferme la conviction avec laquelle ils s'accrochent à cette planche de salut. (*LNR*, p. 204)

There is no predetermined creative method, no deliberate orchestration of theme, no structural patterning, no moulding of poetic vision into artistic designs, but simply the mental movements and spontaneous imaginings which surge up as a safety-raft in a situation of incompatibility and distress: 'Rien de l'imagination volontaire des professionnels. Ni thèmes, ni développements, ni construction, ni méthode. Au contraire la seule imagination de l'impuissance à se conformer' (*LNR*, p. 204). Michaux emphasizes and re-emphasizes this lack of intellectual or artistic control: 'La volonté, mort de l'Art' (*Pass*, p. 87), he writes, or 'la poésie est un cadeau de la nature, une grâce, pas un travail. La seule ambition de faire un poème suffit à le tuer' (see Bertelé, p. 74). In the case of *Mes Propriétés*: 'Même les mots inventés, même les animaux inventés dans ce livre sont inventés "nerveusement" et non constructivement selon ce que je pense, du langage et des animaux' (*LNR*, p. 205). One thinks of Surrealism with its 'absence of control of reason' and unimpeded flow of automatic writing sucking deep from the subconscious to relieve repression and frustration and set up a transfusion between the innermost desires and reality:

> Les morceaux, sans liens préconçus, y furent faits paresseusement au jour le jour, suivant mes besoins, comme ça venait, sans 'pousser', en suivant la vague, au plus pressé toujours, dans un léger vacillement de la vérité, jamais pour construire, simplement pour préserver. (*LNR*, pp. 204–5)

But the intention, that of self-preservation in a situation of conflict, is different, and behind Michaux's 'lazily' engendered or 'involuntary' poetic texts one always senses a watchful, resourceful presence which never sleeps: 'apaisé le maître du clavier feint le sommeil' (*FV*, p. 16).

Michaux's is not a representational but an exploratory art: 'J'écris pour me parcourir. Peindre, composer, écrire: me parcourir. Là est l'aventure d'être en vie' (*Pass*, p. 142). It is an art of the problematical, fluid and adaptable, devoted to questions and not to answers: 'Ce que je voudrais (pas encore ce que je fais) c'est musique pour questionner, pour ausculter, pour approcher le problème d'être' (*Pass*, p. 134). Since understanding comes only after creating—'le vrai poète crée, puis comprend... parfois' (*MM*, p. 66)—the poem is an enigmatic configuration. It proposes a world of signs, and not of explanations or moralistic oversights. It does not seek an artificial unity, but only to reflect the truly mobile, metamorphic nature of a reality in which the self is not a single reliable identity but a 'position d'équilibre' (*Pl*, p. 213) among a host of possible selves, in which a fully formulated conscious thought is only the thin, stiff crust which has coagulated over a vast and turbulent thinking flux. So, 'Signes, symboles, élans, chutes, départs, rapports, discordances, tout y est pour rebondir, pour chercher, pour plus loin, pour autre chose' (*Pl*. p. 216). It is a poetry of instability and multiplicity: 'Signes des dix mille façons d'être en équilibre dans ce monde mouvant qui se rit de l'adaptation' (*FV*, p. 20); a language agile and expansive enough to move among those '*pré-*

gestes en soi, beaucoup plus grands que le geste, visible et pratique qui va suivre' (*FV*, p. 18); a language which refuses the fixed, the established, the symmetrical, the abstract, the classified and plunges into the disordered, pulsating movements of the unknown:

> Signes
> non de toit, de tunique ou de palais
> non d'archives et de dictionnaire du savoir
> mais de torsion, de violence, de bousculement
> mais d'envie cinétique.
>
> (*FV*, p. 19)

As such, it cannot accept the artifices of prosody and the principles of harmonic order which freeze poetic experience into a posture. He plays his tom-tom in rhythmic revolt 'Contre l'alexandrin' and '*Contre le Nombre d'Or*' (*Pass*, pp. 135–7). He leaves behind all abstract calculation and plunges into a tempo which knows no restraining structure:

> Abstraction de toute lourdeur
> de toute langueur
> de toute géométrie
> de toute architecture
> abstraction faite, VITESSE!
>
> (*FV*, p. 14)

It is a poetry of the unfinished, not simply in the sense of incessant departure and re-departure, but in that it attempts to solve the dilemma that any written text is an abandonment of the infinity of 'le penser' and the finite crystallization within words of 'une pensée', a disengagement from the movement, contradiction and uncertainty of the unthinkable mental cosmos and a grateful retreat into the illusion of completeness. Michaux chooses as the epigraph to his collection *Passages*, a title which itself speaks of journeys rather than arrivals, the following translation from the fourteenth-century Japanese writer Yoshida No Kaneyoshi:

Koyu, le religieux, dit: seule une personne de compréhension réduite désire arranger les choses en séries complètes.

C'est l'incomplétude qui est désirable. En tout, mauvaise est la régularité.

Dans les palais d'autrefois, on laissait toujours un bâtiment inachevé, obligatoirement.

It is for this reason that the author favours such titles as *Vers la sérénité* and *Vers la complétude*, stressing continued 'movement towards' rather than finality, and covets the fluid potential of music, 'opération du devenir, opération humaine la plus saine' (*Pass*, p. 184). What he goes on to say of music is the perfect summary of his own poetics: 'Art des générosités, non des engagements. Art des horizons et de l'expansion, non des enclos. Art dont le message partout ailleurs serait utopie. *Art de l'élan*' (*Pass*, p. 185). It is remarkable how many times Michaux calls on the architectural parallel to illustrate his ideal of an 'imperfect' poetry which refuses the living death of false order and the final version. Speaking of the ability of music to mould itself to the complex, variable continuum of 'la vie intérieure', he writes:

> Ici sont exposés ses tâtonnements, ses hésitations, ses brusqueries, ses accentuations, ses brouillons, ses reprises, ses retours en arrière que les autres arts tiennent soigneusement cachés (comme ce serait émouvant, pourtant, de trouver tout autour d'une cathédrale, les beaux restes en pierre de tentatives avortées, les ébauches à demi terminées, d'autres menées plus loin mais tout de même arrêtées avant la fin, tous ces commencements de cathédrales se pressant autour de la grande...). (*Pass*, p. 183)

Just as, in spatial terms, the Japanese palace did not imprison the mind within an inalterable harmony but left a void within which it could move and chase an *ailleurs*, so he imagines an art, perhaps more destructive than constructive, which would eschew eternal form and seek to live authentically in time, with all its erasures and resurrections:

> Mais si un architecte construit un château, en le détruisant aussitôt après, même avec des gradations très savantes et originales dans la destruction et la ruine, personne n'appréciera. De même dans un tableau on a coutume, pauvrement, de se contenter de l'état final.
> Aussi des artistes de génie existent peut-être, qu'on ne découvrira que par le cinéma, dans un nouveau genre d'architecture uniquement à filmer, artistes capables de monuments et d'œuvres inouïs 'dans le temps', défaits à mesure en de magnifiques 'retombées'. Des bâtisseurs viendront, de villes fantastiques, bientôt croûlantes et retournées au néant, mais dont les passages resteront dans toutes les mémoires. (*Pass*, p. 150)

The break with Classical aesthetics is absolute. In the violent magnetic field of his own poetic processes, where everything is broken, scattered and twirled according to the new 'infernal rhythms' of a revolutionary art, this is what happens to Classical statues:

J'y mets aussi des statues. Intéressant. Quoique je sois allergique aux statues, surtout aux grecques et aux romaines, j'en mets ici, pièces de choix qui n'ont jamais été à pareil enfer. Eh bien, dans ces moments, sur mon plateau magnétique, on les dirait—c'est extraordinaire—on les dirait émues, elles, ces grandes poseuses immobiles depuis des millénaires, quelque chose passe en elles, presque la vie, quelque chose comme un sentiment secret, comme dix, vingt sentiments secrets se précipitant dessus, ou plutôt dessous, bouleversement que je ne puis voir moi-même sans bouleversement. (*FF*, p. 222)

The poetic act has no one specific function for Michaux. It may be an act of liberation, expansion and release; an act of self-dissolution and self-alleviation; a spanning of the gap between actuality and aspiration, presence and distance; a relief from the asperities and rigidities of reality; or a miraculous access to the true fluidity and movement of the phenomenal world and the intimate 'soft marrow' of things:

Pourquoi faut-il aussi que je compose?
Pour briser l'étau peut-être,
pour me noyer peut-être,
pour me noyer sans m'étouffer,
pour me noyer mes piques,
mes distances, mon inaccessible.
Pour noyer le mal,
le mal et les angles des choses,
et l'impératif des choses,
et le dur et le calleux des choses,
et le poids et l'encombrement des choses,
et presque tout des choses,
sauf le passage des choses,
sauf le fluide des choses,
et la couleur et le parfum des choses,
et le touffu et la complicité parfois des choses.
(*Pass*, pp. 122–3)

It may be to build up his defences or breach those of others; to work a rhythmic spell on his inner forces or on the resistibility of the outside world; to drown out and transcend the importunate presence of others when 'le mal, c'est le rythme des autres'

(*Pass*, p. 135); to explore the voices of his own hidden recesses; to adjust at will his inner tempos and break away from the metronome of mediocrity; to dissociate himself from the anonymity of collective subservience; to guard his equilibrium, with a foot on either side, and be unable to be dislodged:

> Pourquoi je joue du tam-tam maintenant?
> Pour mon barrage
> Pour forcer vos barrages
> Pour franchir la vague montante des nouveaux empêcheurs
> Pour m'ausculter
> Pour me tâter le pouls
> Pour me précipiter
> Pour me ralentir
> Pour cesser de me confondre avec la ville avec EUX avec le
> pays avec hier
> Pour rester à cheval.
>
> (*Pass*, p. 135)

It may be a kind of immediate 'action-writing' to give therapeutic release and clear the clutter which chokes the mental space: 'Ecriture directe enfin pour le dévidement des formes/ pour le soulagement, le désencombrement des images' (*FV*, p. 21). It may be an expurgation of evil humours and a catharsis of the kind felt by Michaux when he hears Chinese melodies (*BA*, p. 153). It may be a cry to over-shout the threatening cries of others or to anaesthetize the acute call of his own pain: 'On crie pour taire ce qui crie' (*FV*, p. 43); or a metamorphic counter-measure to turn the irrefutable evidence of a situation into a harmless illusion and the pressure of a desperate present into a 'has-been': 'Sincère? J'écris afin que ce qui était vrai ne soit plus vrai. Prison montrée n'est plus une prison' (*Pass*, p. 146). In this case there is no question of art as sincere self-expression: for what can be the 'sincerity' of one *ad hoc* measure among many thrown up to protect the self, extricate it, transform a passing danger or volatilize the truth of a transient situation? It may be the means to dissipate a claustrophobic anguish: 'Pour crever mon plafond sans doute surtout j'appelle' (*Pass*, p. 122). It may be an act of relief from the artificiality and tension of preserving a single self, the opportunity of living the multiple lives for which one is really due: 'Dans une double, triple, quintuple vie, on serait plus à l'aise, moins rongé et paralysé du subconscient hostile au conscient (hostilité des autres "moi" spoliés)' (*Pl*, p. 213). It may be an expression of the sheer appetite for invention: 'Dès que j'écris, c'est pour commencer à inventer' (*Pass*, p. 28). It may be writing as unlimited expansion; or writing as a form of short-circuiting, employed to sever oneself from the current of reality, to cut off some mental movement which could become an avalanche and, paradoxically, to halt the march of words themselves: 'Attention au bourgeonnement! Ecrire plutôt pour court-circuiter' (*FV*, p. 50). It may be an abolition of will-power and ordered organization and the willing demolition of his own person:

> Peu ici compose.
> Tout le contraire,
> m'y décompose,
> en paix, en fluide, m'y décompose
> (*Pass*, p. 123)

or it may be a condensation of force and self-control and a fight against dispersion: 'Ecrire, qui demande force, et fait appel à de la force, devient force, devient contrôle, extension de contrôle, adversaire de l'incessante poussiérisation de soi' (*CG*, p. 165). It may be an instinctive rebellion against sensed dictatorships within himself; or a shaking-off of potential dictatorships from the outside. Most often it is a violent exorcism, performed 'pour se délivrer d'emprises' (*EE*, p. 8): a laying of ghosts and haunting obsessions.

But through all these manifestations—and one cannot attribute to Michaux's poetry a simplistic unity of purpose any more than one can allocate his poems to a specific literary genre—it is action and efficacy.

III

THEMES

Revolt, the determination to galvanize himself against compromise and remain unassimilable, is the powerful motor of
Michaux's work. 'Mon salut est dans l'hostilité', he writes. 'Le
difficile est de la garder. Il me faut me recueillir souvent, pour
retrouver le voltage. Mes accus, il y en a de meilleurs' (*Pass*,
p. 105). Admittedly his poetry shows wild oscillations between
excited creativity and fatigue, acts of domination and impotence,
rapid self-projection and relapse, between the bursting shell of
self-transcendence and the flat diarrhoea of self-evacuation and
self-disgust. But there is little wrong with the accumulators of
this poet who sees his reflection in the image of the cactus, the
dagger or the harpoon, conceives of himself as 'l'homme pour
l'opération éclair' (*FV*, p. 10), and writes as his epitaph: 'Qu'il
repose en révolte' (*VP*, pp. 116–18), as if anticipating that he
will leave this world eternally irreconciled.

From the earliest texts, one meets a distinctive charge of
hatred: 'J'ai besoin de haine, et d'envie, c'est ma santé' (*Ec*,
p. 98). It is a hatred with no specific object or orientation, content to disturb, disfigure and demolish with no immediate
thought for construction:

> Il y a haine en moi, forte et de date ancienne,
> Et pour la beauté on verra plus tard
>
> (*LNR*, p. 188)

and

> La rage n'a pas fait le monde
> mais la rage y doit vivre.
>
> (*Pl*, p. 100)

In its ancestry runs Rimbaud's poetic anger. It no doubt gleans
a good deal, too, from the contemporary iconoclasm of Dada and
Surrealism. In the mid-twenties members of the *Révolution
surréaliste* are declaring that 'avant toute préoccupation surréaliste
ou révolutionnaire, ce qui domine dans leur esprit est un

certain état de fureur'.[1] André Breton, for his part, takes pride in
the fact that 'le surréalisme n'ait pas craint de se faire un dogme
de la révolte absolue, de l'insoumission totale, du sabotage en
règle, et qu'il n'attende rien que de la violence'.[2] But Michaux,
though fleetingly tempted by the ideal of a world-wide frater-
nity of 'Camarades du "Non" et du crachat mal rentré', cannot
finally absorb the myth of collective revolt and goes his own
contemptuous way, saying:

> Camarades...mais il n'y a pas de camarades du 'Non'
> Comme pierre dans le puits mon salut à vous!
> Et d'ailleurs, Zut!
>
> (*Pl*, p. 100)

He gives little credence to the shared enthusiasms and wishful
common identity of revolutionary fraternities which, spilling
over into the public arena in exuberant but flaccid *professions de
foi*, dilute authentic revolt to almost nothing:

> J'ai toujours admiré que des gens qui se croient gens de révolution se
> sentissent frères.
> Ils parlaient l'un de l'autre avec émotion: coulaient comme un potage.
> Ce n'est pas de la haine, ça mes amis, c'est de la gélatine.
> La haine est toujours dure,
> Frappe les autres. (*Ec*, p. 100)

As the poet has said, in an interview confirming his almost total
indifference to fashionable literary modes and current influences:
'J'ai l'esprit de révolte, mais absolument pas l'esprit de com-
pétition' (quoted in Bréchon, p. 209).

It is not, then, in the mood of an age but in the nest of his
intimate obsessions that one must seek the origins of Michaux's
hatred. It is inseparable from a sense of personal lack and
deprivation:

> Ce n'est qu'un petit trou dans ma poitrine,
> Mais il y souffle un vent terrible,
> Dans le trou il y a haine (toujours), effroi aussi et impuissance.
>
> (*Ec*, p. 98)

Hatred is the maelstrom which swirls to life in the hollow of
absence and non-fulfilment, in the gap between desire and
possession ('J'ai besoin de haine, *et d'envie...*'), to become a vast
destructive force: 'Mon vide est un grand mangeur, grand

broyeur, grand annihileur' (*Ec*, p. 100). A new voracious successor to Baudelairean *ennui*, it would willingly destroy the universe in the energy of the insatiable. It is an agent of revenge in the absurd confrontation between his own void and the false solidity of the world at large. It is the saving grace which grows from vacuum to vitality and converts nonentity into individual power. Michaux repeatedly reminds one of the sensitive and unsubstantial interior which is the reverse side of hardened revolt:

> Je ne suis en effet devenu dur que par lamelles;
> Si l'on savait comme je suis resté moelleux au fond.
> Je suis gong et ouate et chant neigeux.
>
> (*LNR*, p. 188)

Already in these words there is evidence of a sharply felt division between *l'espace du dehors* and *l'espace du dedans*, and between different levels of expression in the self: at the exterior is the 'sounding brass' of his violent contact with the world of others; behind this lies a nebulous mental matter which absorbs the shocks and allows the consciousness to sink into a more ductile medium; and deep within there is the muted sound of an intimate poetry, with no sharp dissonances, tucked far away from the clanging reverberations where the self meets reality. A similar image is presented in his portrait of the insulated, self-sufficient 'Homme de lettres' (*LNR*, p. 189), whose primitive, derisive language, bursting outwards towards the world in angular and spasmodic formations, forms a protective exterior behind which the inner man savours the serenity of an artificial silence:

> Et encore, il s'engrange qu'il dit,
> Et pète par toutes les fissures.
> En blocs, en lames, en jets et en cristal,
> Mais derrière le mur de ses paroles,
> C'est un grand sourd.

But the relations between resistant exterior and soft marrow, between the obverse and reverse side of the wall of words, are not always so therapeutic. There are times when the weapon of resistance and hostility is a two-edged blade which, as it strikes out, scours the poet's inner space:

> La haine est toujours dure,
> Frappe les autres,

Mais râcle ainsi son homme à l'intérieur continuellement.
C'est l'envers de la haine.
Et point de remède. Point de remède.

(*Ec*, pp. 100-1)

Paradoxically, Michaux thrives on lack and draws strength from pain. He can touch his void as if it were a consistent substance. Were it to disappear, he would be like the man, cured of an ailment, who has nothing left by which to assure himself of his individuality: 'S'il disparaît, ce vide, je me cherche, je m'affole et c'est encore pis' (*Ec*, p. 99). The poet addresses for this reason 'le Malheur', ploughing its debilitating furrow through his being, not only as a haven but as 'Mon avenir, ma vraie mère, mon horizon' (*Pl*, p. 83): a force of genesis opening expanses of possibility and promise. In the text 'Etapes' (*LNR*, pp. 47-8) Michaux recounts how pernicious gods stripped him for a time of his power of misery and misfortune, giving in return a balancing-pole and a new equilibrium with which, in his innocence, he was almost content; but, though he did not stumble or make so many *faux pas*, he could no longer leap and it soon became a death-in-life. For, with 'le malheur', they took his hammer and tools, the means of his personal repair-jobs and creative counter-measures; then came the turn of 'mes chiffons, mes bouteilles cassées, tous les débris', the tattered and broken possessions of his derelict but dynamic existence; and finally it was the departure of his agents of aggression and destruction, his symbols of kinetic force and mobility: the eagle which perched on a dead tree, his lightning-bolts, his teeth and claws. In the same way he refuses the aimlessness, the character-sapping nonentity, of 'Bonheur bête' (*LNR*, p. 49), not thorny enough to snag a single positive word, of which he can only say: 'Il n'a pas de limite, il n'a pas de..., pas de. [...] Il m'enlève tout élan, il ne me laisse ni la vue, ni l'oreille, et plus il...et moins je...'. So it is that he finds ether, with its more 'Christian' procedure of tearing a man violently from himself, more compatible than the 'perfection sans surforce' (*Ec*, p. 106) of opium, which leaves its vague satisfaction lying slackly in the veins: 'Et, mes nerfs étouffés, qu'est-ce qui me reste?' he asks.

Titles such as 'Qu'il repose en révolte' and 'Repos dans le malheur' are a sign that the only authentic rest of which Michaux conceives is one animated by opposition and continuing non-fulfilment. His memory he sees finally inscribed 'dans ce qui cherche et ne trouve pas' and 'dans les bras tordus des désirs à jamais inassouvis' (*VP*, pp. 116–18). In *Un Barbare en Asie* (pp. 43–4) he warns that the age of rest is now over, as much for the individual as for Western European civilization as a whole: 'Mais l'Europe ne peut se reposer sur personne. Et elle ne peut plus se reposer du tout. Le temps du repos est fini'. And, as a revolutionary figure, his own energy is firmly behind the influences of change and flux:

> Ruine au visage aimable et reposé,
> Ruine pour tout dire, ruine.
> (*LNR*, p. 178)

A thread of texts throughout Michaux's work shows the relish with which he shatters stability, turns the established order topsy-turvy and undermines human confidence and pretention. The vision of 'Villes mouvantes' in *Qui je fus* (1927) is one, as the title implies, in which towns, thrown from their bearings, go lurching unpredictably over the face of the globe. It is a miniature allegory similar in certain respects to Camus's *La Peste*: an existential crisis without precedent to which no traditional values correspond and in which men are forced to re-question their relationship with the anti-human accidents of an absurd universe. Official interpreters are pushed on to jutting promontories to make their oracular pronouncements, only to stammer in confusion; doctors stay buried for nights in the Great Medical Encyclopaedia without finding a single comparable case; Captain Sainsbury of the English Navy does his duty, come what may, and lights signal-lamps fore and aft on his ship, in the cathedral and in suburbia; the sons of Missolonghi, the scene of a famous death or glory stand against the Turks, keep a stiff upper lip while thinking above all of honour and their legacy to their children; notaries and bureaucrats, unable to master the mechanics of the parachute, fall to their death from bedroom windows; and self-important *pères de famille* in their impressive buildings stand moaning piteously from behind their lorgnettes. In a more mysterious and unsettling piece of 1936 entitled 'Portrait d'homme' (reprinted in *L'Herne*, pp. 334–9), the author casts himself as 'le grand semeur de découragement', disturbing the habitual motions of the domestic dinner-table with the sudden reflection: 'Je voudrais bien savoir sur quelle vague roule le monde en ce moment'. The result is devastating:

> Chacun s'arrête de manger. Quoique comprenant mal, sa femme, son fils (il n'a que huit ans) et sa petite fille, un peu plus âgée, sont pris de la sale impression que leur vie, mal suspendue, 'bouge'.
> Plus d'appuis.
> Ils se regardent, misérables.

Not yet content and 'ravi d'une situation qui se présente d'elle-même si fausse et mal d'aplomb et conforme à son idée du monde selon quoi tout va de travers', he drives the wedge of his revolutionary speculations even further into the troubled face of local reality, spreading the rumour that preparations are well under way to evacuate Europe and leaving his wife only the precarious consolation that new roads are being driven towards the Caucasus as a means of escape: 'Cet inutile sauvetage, cette perche qu'il lui tendait devenue faible paille, emportée dans le tourbillon général, tout ça est tellement satisfaisant pour sa forme d'esprit, qu'il va se coucher complètement calmé'. The more recent work 'Quelques jours de ma vie chez les insectes' indicates that Michaux has not relinquished the rôle of 'semeur de découragement'. Astride the dangerous and colourful creature of the imagination, he still sows panic through the ranks of humanist security:

> Nous allions aussi à la chasse aux hommes. Des dégénérés!
> En plein vol, moi à califourchon sur le corselet d'une volante à quatre ailes, on vous les cueillait par la tête, tandis qu'ils marchaient avec cette allure patiente, réglée et ridicule qui est la leur et qui pue l'hypocrisie. (*FV*, p. 124)

A small group of poems from *La Nuit remue* (pp. 83–91), 'Contre!', 'Nous autres', 'Comme je vous vois' and 'Le Livre des réclamations', gives a particularly forceful image of the earliest, perhaps most melodramatic, expression of Michaux's revolt. In a spirit reminiscent of Rimbaud's 'Qu'est-ce pour nous, mon cœur, que les nappes de sang', 'Contre', renewing the image of the *poète maudit* ('Frères, mes frères damnés, suivez-moi avec confiance'), rings an emphatic death-knell over the whole of civilization and conjures up forces destructive of tradition, system, sacrosanct objects and values. As the frozen forms of Parthenons and Mings go tumbling, the poet pronounces a new creative

order built on the nebulous, the mobile, the turbulent (one
thinks of Breton's phrase, 'La beauté sera CONVULSIVE ou elle
ne sera pas'):[3]

> Avec de la fumée, avec de la dilution de brouillard
> Et du son de peau de tambour,
> Je vous assoierai des forteresses écrasantes et superbes,
> Des forteresses faites exclusivement de remous et de secousses,
> Contre lesquelles votre ordre multimillénaire et votre géométrie
> Tomberont en fadaises et galimatias et poussière de sable sans raison.

'Nous autres' is a dramatic, self-dramatizing indictment of a life
which has granted the poet nothing but deprivation and frustration. It contains a rather self-pitying attack on injustice and
inequality and its prophecy of a new age, a fanciful utopia
summed up in images of fertility, abundance and impetus has
more than a hint of forced rhetoric. But the poem is interesting
for its picture of a band of 'horribles travailleurs' (cf. Rimbaud's
'Lettre du voyant') doomed to work with the void, to lose all
their stock in a never-ending existential dilapidation, and to
burrow their way with no prospect of arrival in the claustrophobic passages of a world of 'chemins de taupe, de courtilière'.
It is these retributive pariahs who are now putting in their
threatening claim. 'Le Livre de réclamations' continues the
theme: it is at the same time a list of requisitions and a book of
lamentations, compiled by a poet whose violence is in proportion
to his destitution. A poem of tooth and claw, coloured by a 'rage,
rage, sans objet', it sets on stage the shocking irrationality of
aggressive, sadistic instincts suddenly let off the leash. Written
in the same prophetic tone, 'Comme je vous vois', anticipates a
day of reckoning when the great pretence of life will be stripped
by the icy blast of Nothingness, and mocks the hollowness of
social values, notably the wretched perversion of spirituality
which is Christianity: 'Alors ça marche toujours la vente des
timbres pour l'au-delà?' One should add to these four poems
'L'Avenir' (*LNR*, pp. 199–200), more apocalyptic than the others
and especially notable in that it takes the form of an incantatory
spell or malediction: an act of rhythmic and phonetic sorcery.
Words, only half recognizable, are squeezed out in a relentless,
frightening lava-flow swallowing everything in its path, as a
sinister nameless *agent provocateur* laughs in the background:

> Quand les mah,
> Quand les mah,
> Les marécages,
> Les malédictions,
> Quand les mahahahahas,
> Les mahahaborras,
> Les mahahamaladihahas,
> Les matratrimatratrihahas,
> Les hondregordegarderies,
> Les honcucarachoncus,
> Les hordanoplopais de puru para puru,
> Les immoncéphales glossés,
> Les poids, les pestes, les putréfactions,
> Les nécroses, les carnages, les engloutissements,
> Les visqueux, les éteints, les infects... ;

symptoms of pleasure and wishful unity are turned into sources of pain, antagonism, unrest and vertigo:

> Le jus de la joie se changeant en brûlure,
> Les caresses en ravages lancinants, les organes du corps les mieux unis en duels au sabre,
> Le sable à la caresse rousse se retournant en plomb sur tous les amateurs de plage,
> Les langues tièdes, promeneuses passionnées, se changeant soit en couteaux, soit en cailloux... ;

the World, self-enclosed and firmly centred, is pummelled by hostile words and waves of rhythm until its compartments crumble and it is rocked from its pivot; and the ultimate force of destruction, 'l'*Epouvantable-Implacable*', irresistibly invoked, finally descends to leave nothing in its wake but 'Espace! Espace non stratifié...'.

Most significantly, as the beginning of 'L'Avenir' illustrates, Michaux's work is an act of revolt against poetic language itself, against what one might call 'l'odieux compartimentage du langage' (see *Pl*, p. 70). Individual words no longer respect their watertight boundaries but spill out unimpeded, eat into and contaminate each other, form strange new compounds which could proliferate *ad infinitum*. The poem 'Ra' (*LNR*, p. 196) shakes off the strictures of traditional syntax and grammatical links and twists them into new shapes:

> A tant refus secoue l'abeille manège son trou.
> Avec arrêtez-là debout dans rouf-à la rouffarde;

> Des plus, des sautes allégresses, des laisse-moi-assis,
> Des rachète-moi-tout-cru, des libelle-donc-ça-autrement.

Or there may be a more radical reduction to non-sense, in which
language is ripped from its intellectual overlords and allowed to
roam as a primitive force:

> Ou te bourdourra le bodogo,
> Bodogi.
>
> (*LNR*, p. 192)

The same refusal of the petty limits, the tired vocabulary, the
univocal platitudes of expression is evident in 'Le grand combat'
(*Q JF*, p. 74) where one meets a kind of ominous 'Jabberwocky',
sensuously and self-indulgently vicious:

> Il l'emparouille et l'endosque contre terre;
> Il le rague et le roupète jusqu'à son drâle;
> Il le pratèle et le libucque et lui barufle les ouillais;
> Il le tocarde et le marmine,
> Le manage rape à ri et ripe à ra.
> Enfin il l'écorcobalisse.

Much of Michaux's early verse borders on a pre-linguistic blood-
lust. As he says in *Qui je fus* (p. 72): 'ma partie de reins dit "sang"
à ma partie haute et rue à tout ce qui n'est pas injures et viande
fraîche'. These 'mots en liberté' illustrate a violent need to
extricate poetry from the trap of language: its straitjackets, its
clichés, its pale rationality. They are 'signes surtout pour retirer
son être du piège de la langue des autres' (*FV*, p. 20). And whether
the poet holds in his sights the words of others or his own words,
his vigilance and resistance are no less resourceful:

cette fois on ne se laisse plus faire, les mots dans les phrases, les phrases
dans la page, on les bouscule, on les retourne, on les retire, on les
échange, on les recompose, non pour refaire le livre mais pour le défaire,
pour les faire sauter et se dévergonder ailleurs, pour le plaisir pur de la
non-obéissance, de la non-soumission. (*FF*, pp. 203–4)

This, for a poet, is perhaps the supreme revolt.

THE ABSURD

Critics have not always appreciated Michaux's rôle as a key
witness to the existential crisis of the twentieth century. Two
texts in particular, 'Mes Propriétés' (1929) and *Un certain Plume*

(1930, extended edition 1938), depict in distinctive ways the anguish of contemporary man confronted with the absurd.

'Mes Propriétés' (*LNR*, pp. 119–26), like *Qui je fus* before it (1927), poses the question of identity and self-ownership. The words 'mes propriétés' may be taken in two senses: those properties or attributes which make up the specific character of a given body, differentiate it in function from other forms and enable one to speak of it as an autonomous entity; and those properties or possessions which give one material ownership and the illusion, if not of mastery over the phenomenal world, then at least of a well-populated and protected existence with a substantial claim on life. So, when the poet writes: 'Dans mes propriétés tout est plat, rien ne bouge', using the concrete metaphor of lands or property, he refers simultaneously to a problem of self-definition and a problem of possession, to difficulties in his relations with his own inner world, a flat, undifferentiated mass without project or identity, and with reality in general, which refuses to be appropriated and leaves him undernourished.

The text speaks of a personal domain (akin to the world to be inhabited some twenty years later by Beckett's Molloy) which emits signs of life, spasmodic intimations of shape, but from which all adequate explanation or justification is missing. There is no reassurance of a transcendent purpose or presiding principle, nor any hope of an ultimate arrival which might redeem the endless blind burrowing. Here, like a multifarious Tantalus, the poet clutches vainly at solidity and outline, in search of something which would hold together and not fall back into the quagmire of the unnameable:

et si je vois quelque chose émerger, je pars comme une balle et saute sur les lieux, mais la tête, car c'est le plus souvent une tête, rentre dans le marais; je puise vivement, c'est de la boue, de la boue tout à fait ordinaire ou du sable, du sable...

In this state of dispossession and exile, he has often coveted attractive objects from the outside world and sought to transfer them to his own domain, thus proving that there is a correspondence or meaningful transfusion between himself and the world at large. But despite his conscientious efforts to learn all that constitutes the essence of the particular object and create the appropriate environment for its existence within his mental arena, the transfer is always abortive: 'Ma documentation devient de plus en plus vaste. Mais quand j'essaie de le transporter dans ma propriété, il lui manque toujours quelques organes essentiels'. Sartre's distinction between *pour soi* and *en soi* has a bearing here: the picture is partly that of the subjective consciousness aspiring to the quality of 'is-ness' or 'being in itself' which appears to be the property of the object contemplated. But, for the narrator, there remains nothing but 'documentation de plus en plus vaste': an endless experimental 'working towards' which can never attain for itself the wholeness and crystalline contour of what the eye saw and the mind conceived. The absurd thus dogs him in the form of unassimilable material and constant discrepancy. The hope that a creature, once established in his inner universe, might propagate and gradually occupy the vacant space—an image suggesting the desire for a self which would progressively corroborate itself and grow in its own image instead of an unrelated succession of selves, each erasing the other in a mutual indifference —is sadly frustrated: 'quant à se multiplier, sur mes propriétés on ne se multiplie pas, je ne le sais que trop'. Dissolution never becomes evolution. Should he by chance succeed in fashioning some small fragment to set against the fleeting nonentity of existence, then this fragment stands redundant, *de trop*, enjoying no preordained place in a wider pattern of things: 'J'arrive bien à former un objet, ou un être, ou un fragment. Par exemple une branche ou une dent, ou mille branches et mille dents. Mais où les mettre?' It is divorced from all *ensemble*, planted absurdly in a situation to which it has no obvious relevance and where nothing has any conclusive reference to anything else: '...et certains jours dans ma propriété j'ai là cent mille crayons, mais que faire dans un champ avec cent mille crayons? ce n'est pas approprié'. Any acquisition, moreover, is only at the expense of another: as he prepares a jaw for the tooth, and then a digestive and excretory system, in the hope of proving himself equal to creation, the tooth itself disappears and then the jaw and so on in an ever-frustrating cycle. The mind and its artifice can hold no more than one strand of reality while a million others slip away: 'Devant et derrière ça s'éclipse aussitôt, ça ne peut pas attendre un instant'. Seen from a temporal point of view, the narrator's plight is the insecurity of successive immediate presents, coming and going without trace. As Camus writes of *l'homme absurde*: 'Dans un

univers soudain privé d'illusions et de lumières, l'homme se sent
un étranger. Cet exil est sans recours puisqu'il est privé des
souvenirs d'une patrie perdue ou de l'espoir d'une terre promise'[4]
    'Mes Propriétés' stirs many echoes in the corridors of Existen-
tialist thought. It presents an image of life given for nothing,
unsupported and unjustified, which the individual must confront
as a kind of foreign body and attempt to appropriate. He is, as
it were, 'condemned to be free', derelict, abandoned to shape
himself from the void. As Sartre might say, 'l'homme est à faire':
he has no other definition than the need to create his own
definition. In 'Le Portrait de A.' Michaux writes: 'Il se demande
où est sa vie, parfois elle lui paraît en avant, rarement passée
ou actuelle, plutôt à faire' (*Pl*, p. 107). Man is a project pursued
in the dark; he cannot step outside his existence to possess it as
a totality. And just as Mathieu in Sartre's *L'Age de raison* says in a
crisis of self-justification, 'Ma liberté, elle me pèse: voilà des
années que je suis libre pour rien. Je crève d'envie de la troquer
un bon coup contre une certitude',[5] so the narrator of 'Mes
Propriétés' yearns to dry out his unsubstantial marshes, reclaim
his life as solid land and make it habitable:

> Et si je m'obstine, ce n'est pas bêtise.
> C'est parce que je suis condamné à vivre dans mes propriétés et qu'il
> faut bien que j'en fasse quelque chose.
> Je vais bientôt avoir trente ans, et je n'ai encore rien; naturellement je
> m'énerve.

But 'Mes Propriétés' represents both a *crise de conscience* and a *prise
de conscience*. Sick of piecemeal constructions which disappear like
water through the vessels of the Danaides, the protagonist deter-
mines to undertake the most fundamental *table rase*: 'Alors je
supprime tout et il n'y a plus que les marais, sans rien d'autre,
des marais qui sont ma propriété et qui veulent me désespérer'.
This is by no means the only work in modern literature depicting
an anguished reduction to nothing as the preliminary to an
elaboration of personal values. Sartre says: 'La vie humaine
commence de l'autre côté du désespoir';[6] and it is only through a
long familiarity with universal indifference, followed by a confrontation with the senseless negation of human life in its absolute
form, that Camus's *étranger*, Meursault, can finally grasp his
individuality and affirm himself as a value. Michaux's narrator,

estranged from the life and values of others and finding nothing outside but the irreconcilable, retreats to his own poor property and discovers that it *does* exist: 'mes propriétés qui ne sont rien, mais qui représentent quand même du terrain familier, et ne me donnent pas cette impression d'*absurde* que je trouve partout'. However yielding or vacuous, it provides an authentic ground on which to found a sense of identity. As Michaux states elsewhere:

> Et c'est ma vie, ma vie par le vide.
> S'il disparaît, ce vide, je me cherche, je m'affole et c'est encore pis.
> (*Ec*, p. 99)

The feeling cannot be intellectually justified, but there is a sense of ownership which makes it impossible for him to fall into the undifferentiated mass of others or into total personal nonentity: 'Il y a mon terrain et moi; puis il y a l'étranger'. 'Mes Propriétés' thus represents an anguished conquest of the *moi* as a meaningful value (never an easy process in Michaux's poetry where the self is not an automatic possession and the individual is liable to be swallowed up by other persons, animal forms or indifferent forces: the final words of 'En vérité' (*LNR*, p. 181) are a self-reinforcing act of affirmation:

> C'est moi qui...
> Ce sont les autres qui ne pas...;

while the small determined voice of 'Immense voix' (*EE*, p. 12) has to chant 'je, j'ai, j'suis', like an elementary lesson, to prove its autonomy). The text ends on a strongly positive note:

> Revenons au terrain. Je parlais de désespoir. Non, ça autorise au contraire tous les espoirs, un terrain. Sur un terrain, on peut bâtir, et je bâtirai. Maintenant j'en suis sûr. Je suis sauvé. J'ai une base.

Un certain Plume (*Pl*, pp. 135–76) is unusual in Michaux's writing in that it sets on stage a fictional character, a strange whimsical cross-breed between Charlie Chaplin and Kafka's K. or Camus's Meursault, whose tragi-comic misfortunes and discomfitures we follow through an inconsequential succession of situations not of his own making. (One should add, however, that even the first-personal *je* of 'Mes Propriétés' is not Michaux but a transposition: a fictional narrator set apart in an imaginative dimension.) The Plume texts illustrate admirably Camus's definition of the absurd as 'ce divorce entre l'homme et sa vie, l'acteur et son décor',[7] and draw a character who is 'étranger aux autres et à lui-même'.[8] The first piece 'Un Homme paisible' shows Plume living in a world of dreamy distraction, at best mildly astonished by the gratuitous events which take place around him, but usually neutralizing them in an unruffled matter-of-factness. He reaches out of bed to find that the wall of the house has disappeared: ' "Tiens, pensa-t-il, les fourmis l'auront mangé..." et il se rendormit'. He hears a train bearing down on himself and his wife: ' "De l'air pressé qu'il a, pensa-t-il, il arrivera sûrement avant nous" et il se rendormit'. His wife's body is cut to shreds and there is blood all over him: he would have preferred it not to happen, but since it has he can only shrug his shoulders and go back to sleep. The accidents of reality, all equally absurd, sink senselessly into his mattress of indifference and passivity. He sees no reason to intervene. Reality, for its part, does not reach him and register: his 'cut-off' mechanism functions perfectly. The figure of the judge looms up finally and, like Meursault at his trial, Plume is called on to give rational justification to what had none; to account for actions which were foreign to him and for which he can feel no responsibility. Also like Meursault, he is condemned to death. His final response is different, however:

—L'exécution aura lieu demain. Accusé, avez-vous quelque chose à ajouter?
—Excusez-moi, dit-il, je n'ai pas suivi l'affaire. Et il se rendormit.

The matter of life or death is equally indifferent and even to the last he remains detached from his own life, a sleepy foreigner to himself. 'Plume au restaurant' depicts the featherweight hero more obviously in conflict with external reality in the form of organized society: not as a rebel, but as a bemused and apologetic outsider totally unfamiliar with the customs and expectations of an uncompromising environment. If he had some illumination of the principles governing the world in which he finds himself, then he could no doubt put an end to his embarrassing alienation. In the meantime he can only fall foul of some impenetrable law and be innocently guilty. 'Je n'arrive pas à me pénétrer de l'esprit des Lois', writes the narrator of 'Mon Roi' (*LNR*, p. 15). It all begins with a lamb-chop in a restaurant, when the head waiter's

voice murmurs ominously: 'Ce que vous avez là dans votre
assiette ne figure *pas* sur la carte'. Plume makes profuse apologies,
trying invention after invention in the vain attempt to make peace
with a reality which refuses to budge, condemning himself all
the more as he does so. He is passed from one anonymous social
personage to another, each with an official label and an un-
questionable representative value—head waiter, hotel proprietor,
police inspector, chief of the Special Branch—while he alone is
without a rôle, flaccid and unjustified. Again like Meursault,
what are for him things of the moment, with no further repercussions or implications, become for others a meaningful chain
of consequences, a damning causality from which he cannot be
allowed to escape. His life must be made to yield more in terms
of significance and explanation than it in fact contains: 'Expli-
quez-vous une bonne fois. C'est votre seule chance de salut'.
Once more the trial for an unknown, inconceivable crime is
chosen as an image of human life: indeed, if Plume *could* explain
himself, he would find salvation. The passage 'Plume voyage'
highlights the appropriateness of the hero's name. The unassum-
ing *voyageur sans bagages* is tossed about like a feather in a land
where he has no rights but only obligations, in a system where
everything has been engineered for the regular members and
outsiders cannot be accommodated. People wipe their hands on
him; he is refused hotel accommodation and turned out on the
streets; he is thrown from trains not designed to serve him; he is
denied access to the Coliseum for fear that it will crumble at his
touch. He thus makes no lasting contact with reality and comes
away from places wondering if he has ever been. And yet, like an
infinitely pliable Sisyphus, he continues rolling his life with no
hope of arrival: 'Mais il ne dit rien, il ne se plaint pas. Il songe
aux malheureux qui ne peuvent pas voyager du tout, tandis que
lui, il voyage, il voyage continuellement'. In 'Dans les apparte-
ments de la reine' Plume is a foreigner in courtly society, ill at
ease, ignorant of conventions. As in the other texts, having no
conviction or certainty of his own on which to rely, he acquiesces
to the pressures and persuasions of external reality, only to be
caught in a fatal *engrenage* which pulls him beyond his control.
He is invited to enter the Queen's bedroom (to avoid getting lost
in the kitchens), to take off his clothes (to relieve himself from the
unbearable heat), to touch her right breast (in order to inspect a

curious birth-mark on which she would like his objective foreigner's comments), to caress her legs (otherwise she tends to be terribly distracted)—at which moment the King comes in! Plume has been misled by appearances, thrown quite innocently into a situation of contradiction and conflict, and stained with the guilt of the absurd ('le péché sans Dieu'[9] is Camus's phrase for it), the bemused victim of an irrational world. A further passage deserves mention for its treatment of the theme of death: 'La Nuit des Bulgares'. Again the hero finds himself on an obscure journey among foreigners. But instead of 'de-fusing' the situation by a passive detachment, levity or apologetic pliability, Plume shoots the Bulgarians in a fit of discomfort and suspicion. From that moment, the consequences of his act become a terrible encumbrance: the guard asks for more room to be made in the compartment and Plume is forced to huddle up against the dead bodies; cold heads loll against his neck through the night; the jolting train makes the corpses jog as if they were alive; new passengers who come in must be convinced, by some impossible art of pretence, that nothing is amiss. The image reflects the doubts and guilt of social alienation. But it reflects equally a metaphysical anguish: the senseless and importunate presence of death which frustrates all one's efforts to disguise it, explain it away and somehow clear one's name with regard to it. The question is: how can one live life without dragging the contradiction of death self-consciously along with it?

Taken collectively, the pieces of *Un certain Plume* illustrate graphically the truth of the epigraph to 'La Nuit des embarras' (*Pl*, p. 118):

> Dans cet univers, il y a peu de sourires.
> Celui qui s'y meut fait une infinité de rencontres qui le blessent.

Both 'Mes Propriétés' and *Un certain Plume*, however, are expressions of despair and artistic exorcisms of that despair. In the case of 'Mes Propriétés', a jerky, understated ironic humour makes the narrator a bizarrely entertaining character in his own right. As for Plume, he is more emphatically a 'personnage-tampon' (*Pass*, p. 154), a protective buffer, a source of ingenuous humour, illogicality and farcical mishaps, a character who, in absorbing 'the slings and arrows of outrageous fortune' with such rare equanimity, saves the author himself from excessive distress:

'Dès que j'avais trouvé un personnage (que j'avais "reculé" en lui), j'étais tiré d'embarras, de souffrance (du moins du plus gros, du plus intolérable)' (*Pass*, p. 154). In this way the two texts dramatize the absurd and simultaneously draw its sting.

No study of alienation or dispossession in Michaux's work would be complete without consideration of his view of the nature of the self. The title piece of the poet's *Qui je fus* (1927) gives a starting-point. It presents a lively picture of inner turmoil, conflict of voices, innumerable fragmentary or potential personalities demanding to take precedence, so that the would-be narrator, undermined in his artificial rôle, hardly knows in which voice to recognize himself: 'Je suis habité; je parle à qui-je-fus et qui-je-fus me parlent. Parfois, j'éprouve une gêne comme si j'étais étranger. Ils font à présent toute une société et il vient de m'arriver que je n'entends plus moi-même' (*QJF*, p. 9). Michaux's important Postface to *Plume* (*Pl*, pp. 211–16) reinforces this view of the self as neither a unity nor a constant. It is simply a point of balance, a momentary equilibrium adopted among the turbulent forces of the personality: 'Il n'est pas un moi. Il *n'est pas dix moi. Il n'est pas de moi. MOI n'est qu'une position d'équilibre.* (Une entre mille autres continuellement possibles et toujours prêtes)'. It is always provisional and unstable, subject to changing circumstances which can liberate a latent persona or modify an existing one. It is always an obscure amalgam, fed from many sources, which cannot be said to belong to the individual or faithfully reflect him: it contains a host of impulses and tendencies, some imitative, some counter-reactive; some ready-made, some spontaneously inventive. The poet cannot therefore claim that he belongs to himself. He is a populace: 'Foule, je me débrouillais dans ma foule en mouvement' (*Pl*, p. 214). With each thought and at every single instant he remains a populace, constantly reminded of the discrepancy between a moment's thought as captured and expressed and the real flux and multiplicity of the seething self. Nothing can be circumscribed: reality, not least one's own mental reality, runs away from any momentary expression of it, which stands there false and redundant. It is little wonder that Michaux should see himself as 'un être mille fois biffé' (*VP*, p. 88) and live in permanent contact with 'cette couche en soi, où ne vit plus aucune certitude' (*FV*, p. 77).

Small wonder, too, that he never succeeds in convincing himself of anything which adds up to a life:

> Voulez-vous que je vous dise? Je suis une bonne pompe. Les impressions les plus fortes, les plus vitales ne tiennent pas longtemps. Je les refoule au profit des suivantes et les oublie, et il en est ainsi des autres dans la suite, et puis encore de celles-ci pareillement. On dit que je compte déjà un certain nombre d'années. Je n'ai jamais eu dans ma vie plus de quinze jours, voilà toute ma vie. (*Ec*, p. 71)

DREAM AND NIGHTMARE

Michaux's poetry provides one of the richest stores of image in modern French literature—image not in the sense of individual simile or metaphor, but as what Rimbaud calls the 'Rêve intense et rapide':[10] dense, independent imaginative structures which challenge reason and force the mind to make the dangerous leap between familiar appearances and obscure implications, the explicable and the inexplicable, reality and surreality. Michaux's autobiographical notes tell of the impact upon him of his first French composition: 'Un choc pour lui. Tout ce qu'il trouve en son imagination!' (Bréchon, p. 17). It is a surprise and shock, provoked by the encounter with the foreign products of his imagination and subconscious, which has lost none of its vigour over the years.

The attraction of dream for Michaux, whether night-dream or waking dream, has many facets. It is partly that to liberate the unknown in oneself is to liberate oneself from the unknown: to exteriorize one's hidden obsessions and pin them to the page is an act of self-discovery and self-conquest. Moreover, his concept of the human self as a mere semblance, a false point of balance, leads him to explore dream as an escape from its impoverishment and artificial tension. Pursuing Rimbaud's question: 'Vite! est-il d'autres vies?'[11] he writes: 'Dans une double, triple, quintuple vie, on serait plus à l'aise, moins rongé et paralysé de subconscient hostile au conscient (hostilité des autres "moi" spoliés)' (*Pl*, p. 213). Dream-images take revenge against censorship, releasing and arranging in intriguing patterns the dissimulated matter, giving visual expression to the unconfessable. For this reason, they are a form of revolt more radical and authentic than that of the 'récriminateurs' and 'grands indignés de l'époque' whose

revendications, couched in deliberate rhetoric and still attached
to a life-line of faith and idealism, bear no comparison with 'les
façons secrètes, personnelles, malsonnantes et traîtresses' (*FF*,
p. 183) of the dark world of the night-dreamer. Similarly, where
the images of traditional poetry seek to show language off to its
best advantage, seducing the reader by style and drawing him
into an 'atmosphère de flatterie', those of dream make no con-
cessions, perform only an undermining operation and plunge
one into an 'atmosphère de dévalorisation'. Indifferent to all
questions of *bienséance* and self-respect, they have a taste for
profanation. Free from the scruples of the social *moi* and the con-
ceptual stiffness of the reasoning mind, they are no longer
'images sous surveillance' (*FF*, p. 184), but a roving, rebounding
language of analogy and enigma. This language of immediate
movement and action, as opposed to one of words, has special
appeal for a poet like Michaux: 'Pour moi, après tant d'années,
le rêve assouvit encore un désir inapaisé de mouvements,
d'intenses, excessifs mouvements, me faisant vivre surtout de
gestes, de rythmes, d'actes' (*FF*, p. 206).

Though the definition of the word *âme* may have changed,
Michaux has gone further than any contemporary poet along
the road recommended by Rimbaud: 'La première étude de
l'homme qui veut être poète est sa propre connaissance, entière;
il cherche son âme, il l'inspecte, il la tente, il l'apprend'.[12] He has
cultivated to an extraordinary degree the ability to abandon the
premier moi while remaining self-aware, to be pulled into the
currents of vision while standing back as his own dispassionate
analyst, to relinquish the will and the consciousness while
remaining vigilant and quick to respond: a feat which prompts
him to say with surprise: 'L'endormi, le rêveur que je suis avait
sans le savoir été simultanément prodigieusement alerte, rapide.
Musard, paresseux je n'en avais pas moins été diligent, et
prospecteur, et fouilleur, et explorateur' (*GE*, p. 11). Even so,
it would be wrong to think of Michaux as the proficient controller
of his waking dreams and mental images. More often than not,
they are born of fatigue, physical illness and the lapses of the
feverish mind. The act of writing then becomes an urgent attempt
to limit their encroachments and restore a balance. The experimenter can turn victim and lucidity lose its footing in unreason
and fear. The question which is asked of two nomadic figures

appearing among Michaux's 'Dessins commentés' (*LNR*, pp. 45–6) could be asked of the poet's own dual personality as it travels strangely through the expanses of his *lointain intérieur* and its inner spectacle: 'Est-ce pour regarder qu'ils sont venus sur cette page ces deux-là? Ou pour s'effrayer, pour être glacés d'épouvante à cet étrange spectacle qu'ils voient, qu'ils sont seuls à voir?'

The dream-images which spill on to the pages of *La Nuit remue* (1935) or *Apparitions* (1946) share the same striking characteristics. They are sudden and immediate, bursting on to the stage without a word of warning and from no apparent origin; they have a dynamism and rapidity of development which cannot be held in check; they have a pictorial vividness which makes Michaux the most vigorous and startling *voyant* of the century; and, far from being abstract or purely 'mental', they create a physical impact enlisting all the sensations. They are marked by what the poet calls an 'imperturbable indépendance' (*FF*, p. 130), going their own way with utter disregard for the individual's personal concerns and preferences. They are almost invariably incongruous in that they expose, while doing nothing to resolve, the absurd rift between a man and himself. They do their work by a process, at times frightening, of exaggeration or amplification: 'l'imagination malade...ne fait jamais trop petit, jamais, jamais' (*Pl*, p. 61). They are mobile and ephemeral, resisting any attempt to give them a stable definition (hence the importance for the author of the word *passages*): 'Personne ne peut savoir ce qu'il *y a* dans le subconscient, mais seulement ce qui y *passe* à un moment donné' (*IT*, p. 220). They are multiple and metamorphic, always ready to change their composition and take an unexpected turn: Michaux speaks of the dangers, under the influence of hashish, of mental 'Carrefours à nouvelles déviations possibles' (*IT*, p. 230) and of the menace, not so much of apparitions in themselves, but of 'l'apparition potentielle partout possible, partout capable de surgir, de se manifester davantage' (*GE*, p. 170).

Before studying more closely the moving constellations of images which trace such provocative patterns through Michaux's work, one should insert a reminder not to classify and interpret them too readily. Although he has said:

Un écrivain, il semble, n'a pas besoin de plus d'un sentiment majeur. Amour, ou envie, ou peur, avec les ligatures profondes et multiples d'un bon complexe de base, avec ça il peut aller. Mais il lui en faut un. Sur cette onde il module les autres et tout son univers. C'est *le sentiment porteur...* (*Pass*, p. 147)

and although it is clear that certain recurrent obsessions give his work its tension, he has taken great pains to ensure (by mystification, humour, ambiguity or sheer vitality) that we cannot isolate his 'bon complexe de base' or unify his work falsely around any one 'sentiment porteur'. He deplores, furthermore, that 'une certaine psychologie des profondeurs veut que tous les rêves soient profonds' (*FF*, p. 161): perhaps they are multiple rather than deep, fed from innumerable untraceable sources. To an account of one of his own dreams depicting him among a pride of lions, he adds this salutory footnote:

Toujours suspects pour moi, les grands symboles, comme les idées toutes faites, comme les principes, les généralités évidentes...

Des lions, il faut voir quel genre de lion, lion de place publique, lion pour avancer façon lion, lion grâce à la chevelure qui se veut crinière, lion celui qui simplement veut être servi le premier. Tant qu'on ne sait pas de quel lion il est question, convenablement situé, décrit, on ne sait rien. Non situé, c'est trop facile ensuite de le relier à tout ce qu'on veut. Dire symbole, c'est s'illusionner. (*FF*, pp. 118-19)

Indeed there is no doubt that one of the attractions for him of the dream-image is that savoured by an Arab sage: 'Alors pourquoi vouloir à tout prix interpréter? Un sage arabe répond: "Un rêve non interprété ressemble à un oiseau qui plane au-dessus de la maison, sans se poser" ' (*FF*, p. 163).

The image of the king provides a provocative point of departure: 'commencement sans fin de ma vie obscure' (*LNR*, p. 14). In many texts a royal figure presides obscurely over the poet's tentative life as if challenging its rights, worth and potency. The unfortunate Plume is caught *in flagrante delicto* in the Queen's bedchamber by the King himself. The most complex elaboration, however, is found in the piece called 'Mon Roi' (*LNR*, pp. 13-19) which begins: 'Dans ma nuit j'assiège mon Roi, je me lève progressivement et je lui tords le cou'. In his inner darkness the poet shakes him until his crown topples, strangles him only to see the blue face come back to life, farts vehemently in the royal visage

and laughs derisively in the vain attempt to degrade its impassive
majesty; but the result is always the same:

Et si je me retourne, sa face imperturbable règne, toujours.
Je le gifle, je le gifle, je le mouche ensuite par dérision comme un
enfant.
Cependant il est bien évident que c'est lui le Roi, et moi son sujet, son
unique sujet.

It is the King, moreover, who ensures that figures entering the
poet's room only do so in incomplete and unsubstantial form: a
deflated elephant or a rhinoceros floating like a thin fog. He is
the force which reigns supreme over the fragmentation and
weakness of the poet's life and guarantees their perpetuation:
not simply a symbol of authority, but a symbol of perfection to
which his life is sacrificed in advance and in the face of which his
imaginative efforts will always be ill-formed and provisional. A
closely related regal personage, described as 'l'unique, le Roi au
cerveau-Œil', appears in 'Ceux qui sont venus à moi' (*EE*,
pp. 43–4): possibly the representative of an ideal of self-contained
roundness and unity which probes human duality and calls it
into question. The image of the king fuses with that of the judge.
Not only does Plume find himself continually at odds with forces
of the law, but both the king-figures mentioned take on the
appearance of judges: the former intervenes in the trial of his
wayward subject, not by justifying him, but by reiterating the
arguments of the prosecution; while the latter makes way for 'le
Prince-*juge* à l'œil unique'. At other times it is a Father, an
'immense père reconstruit géant' (*EE*, p. 12) such as that whose
voice he has to blot out in 'Immense voix'. It is then only a step
to images of a loss of status or personal degradation. 'Déchéance'
(*LNR*, pp. 52–3) tells of his 'royaume perdu': once a 'Royaume
superbe' encompassing almost the entire earth, it is now a patch
of ground no bigger than a pin-head with which he scratches
himself on occasions (and presumably pricks his conscience).
The major text 'Fin d'un domaine' (*FV*, pp. 200–17) depicts a
protagonist, master and slave of a disintegrating estate, who fights
a losing battle to maintain the perfect circular perimeter of
hedges and boundary-stones, now barely able to convince himself
of his titles of nobility. Relevant to both passages are these words
from Michaux's portrait of A.: 'ainsi la notion du paradis perdu
et de la chute de l'homme lui était profondément nécessaire'

(*Pl*, p. 111). From judgment, downfall and guilt, one passes to
the ineffaceable stain and images of blood. The dream-hero of
'Vision' (*Pl*, pp. 19–20), having rolled up his sleeves and soaped
his arm until it is rich with lather, then cracks it off on the edge
of the sink in disgust before soaping another arm which has grown
in its place: a procedure repeated seventeen times before he
finally abandons hope of the impossible purification, accepts 'les
mains sales', and disappears with his eighteenth arm, preferring
to leave it unwashed and use it for the needs of the day ahead.

There is an extensive area of images of aggression and violence:
eiderdowns which cry and bleed, a baby's face clawed by a cat,
blood seeping across the picture with its enigmatic seriousness.
One meets an unprecedented range of angular, often metallic,
instruments (broken bottles, splinters of bone, knives, swords,
sabres, thermocauteries, trepans, syringes, saws, drill-heads,
insects' stings or egg-laying tubes), all eager to victimize the poet
and breach his integrity, leaving him severed, mutilated or
porous: 'Là, je subis l'assaut du sabre ondulant…Et avec quelle
souplesse, il entre dans les chairs' (*VP*, p. 55); 'comme c'est
misérable, une poitrine sous une scie qui approche imperturbable' (*VP*, pp. 59–60); or, in the case of the thermocautery, 'Si
exaltant dans le "Je-tu", il est terrible dans le "Tu-moi", ou
même dans le "Je-moi", si vous êtes assez faible pour vous laisser
aborder' (*VP*, p. 54). Persecution is the law of Michaux's mental
world. It is almost inevitably the sign of an upset balance of
power: 'Impuissance, puissance des autres' (*Pl*, p. 57). It may
produce the humorous vision of party-guests beating him over the
head with massive Chianti bottles, a reflection of his social
diffidence, or a gigantic wheel rolling relentlessly to crush him,
an image of totalitarian threat. It may be a terrifying picture of
imminent rape, as when a hook-billed bird of prey avidly contemplates the body of a woman arched on a cross in a forest
clearing, or when the poet himself, falling into some grotesque
mental arena, knows that he is 'désirable comme une jeune vierge
en robe transparente dans une caserne de troupiers' (*Pl*, p. 57).
Or it may be an image where victimization and void come
together, eliciting the remark: 'Mais les ennemis que j'ai ne
sont pas des corps à battre, car ils manquent totalement de corps'
(*LNR*, p. 117). But all illustrate the same awareness: 'Impression
de la présence de l'autre, de la poussée de l'autre, de l'empiétement

de l'autre. L'autre ressenti comme danger, comme attaquant, poursuivant, voulant agir sur soi' (*GE*, p. 171). The image of the face,[13] and particularly the eye, has a special value within the theme of persecution. The Eye probes into one across the distance, violates one's inner space, demoralizes and dissolves without absorbing any riposte: 'Qui dira le poids des regards dans la vie?' (*VP*, p. 90); 'Des regards, même en photos, on est sans défense devant eux' (*GE*, p. 170). Michaux's poetry is full of foreign presences seeking their salvation through another being, on the look-out for someone *disponible* on whom to disburden their difficulties, solitude or aggression. Sometimes they are his own inner men rather than dominators from the outside, belonging to the 'Je-moi' rather than the terrible 'Tu-moi', but still taking advantage of a situation of weakness. There are the 'hommes en fil' (*EE*, pp. 33–6) who riddle his interior, or the horde of 'ceux qui sont venus à moi' (*EE*, pp. 43–5): 'Maigres, impropres à la vie, creusés par la recherche, hommes de nulle part'. Such apparitions may not openly persecute but, in soliciting some obscure alliance, cast into doubt one's personal unity and stability. Some are quite alien and incompatible, such as the man who, as soon as the poet closes his eyes, sits opposite him at table and devours in bestial fashion: 'Mais entre lui et moi, rien' (*LNR*, p. 23). Others, with a mysterious affinity, act as a more obvious *alter ego*: the man with his 'petit animal mange-serrure' (*Pl*, p. 21) who walks the dream-corridors of hotels but with whom no pact is finally made, or the 'violon-girafe' (*Pl*, pp. 90–1) with its 'je ne sais quoi, qui nous unit, tragique, et nous sépare'. Others are problematic doubles or projections of himself, drawing the comment: 'Quel drôle de Narcisse je fais' (*VP*, p. 112): a masochistic Narcissus turning the blade inwards as he battles with his own images, locked in a relationship with himself but not one of self-love. All serve to sap the sense of identity and give point to the lament: 'J'étais autrefois si bien fermé!' (*LNR*, p. 113).

From the idea of threatened identity one slips towards images of insecurity, unsubstantiality and void. A liquid blob drops from the ceiling and turns into a woman who flattens out like a pancake, unable to move; a lion staggers into the room, flopping 'comme un vieux paquet de hardes' (*LNR*, p. 17), followed by an elephant like a punctured balloon. As for the poet himself:

J'ai rarement rencontré dans ma vie des gens qui avaient besoin comme moi d'être regonflés à chaque instant.

On ne m'invite plus dans le monde. Après une heure ou deux...voilà que je me chiffonne. Je m'affaisse, je n'y suis presque plus, mon veston s'aplatit sur mon pantalon aplati. (*LNR*, p. 103)

In a spiritual rather than social and physical realm, the same image recurs: 'Je n'avais plus qu'une jambe de pantalon d'âme et elle flottait' (*VP*, p. 94). Bodies which are a precarious amalgam of substance and space, outline and fragmentation, shape and shapelessness, affect his vision: 'Dentelé et plus encore en îles, grand parasol de dentelles et de mièvreries, et de toiles arach-néennes est son grand corps impalpable' (*LNR*, p. 42). Eerie hostile forces declare their intention to interfere with their victim's time mechanism, turning his neat span of days and weeks into a chaos of disintegration and collapse: 'Comme un filet mal conçu, tout s'écoulera entre ses mailles, il n'en subsistera autant dire rien' (*FV*, p. 95). The poet contemplates the superficial 'masques du vide' while feeling through their flimsy membrane the more absolute 'succion effroyable du Vide' (*EE*, pp. 27–8). The wind of the Andes blows to infinity through the hole in his chest. Characters tumble through the endless stages of a nameless abyss. Souls wander indeterminately through 'l'espace aux ombres' (*FV*, pp. 167–94). If a slender life-line is broken, one can be doomed to roam forever 'entre centre et absence'. Michaux's visionary world is the prey of vertigo: the heaving motions of the sea, suddenly exaggerated, leave the onlooker with the ground slipping from under his feet; the man lying in bed feels his stomach drawn into a spin like a wild top; a tiny moving particle can set off an avalanche and a mere *frisson* become a massive enveloping rhythm. It is a world of 'mauvais équilibres', where things are only experienced at the expense of all stability and the poet's life is a frantic, inventive balancing-act. It is also a world of uncontrollable metamorphosis. Michaux gives the key when he says: 'Dès que vous avez perdu votre centre en vous, vous pourrez aussi bien qu'homme, être crapaud' (*VP*, p. 113): when, in a centrifugal world, one's inner lines of force are scattered and the effort to preserve the convenient fiction of a human identity is no longer possible, one can become anything. A piece entitled 'Encore des changements' (*LNR*, pp. 129–33) shows a narrator who, losing the boundaries of his body, is plunged into an absurd succession of transformations: column of ants, boa constrictor, bison, rhombohedron, whale, harpooner, then (as the harpoon is launched) back to whale, boat breaking up, cable, plank and so on. With no adhesion to what could be called his own centre, his identification with each passing image is immediate and total; he runs the gauntlet of shapes, sizes, functions and existences (as if with no claim to an existence of his own); he is used and re-used in a series of bewildering 'ensembles baroques', subjected to speeds, rhythms and modes of apprehension not his own. 'Naissance' (*Pl*, pp. 123–5) gives a similar picture of the character Pon born and reborn *ad infinitum*, knowing nothing but provisional manifestations, substitutions and eclipses.

Images of the body stand out forcibly in the work of this 'malade distingué' (Bréchon, p. 11), illustrating in their own way the theme of 'mauvais équilibres': 'Ainsi je circulais en angoisse dans mon corps affolé, excitant des chocs, des arrêts, des plaintes. J'éveillai les reins, et ils eurent mal. Je réveillai le colon, il pinça; le cœur, il dégaina' (*VP*, p. 52). The heart is a special source of anxiety. Michaux describes what he calls 'la plus imprégnante, la plus désarmante, la plus indigeste émotion de ma vie' (*Pass*, p. 12): hearing his heart-beat, with its listless and irregular thump, on a cardiometer and realizing that his whole life hinged on a little pump of muscle at the mercy of a moment's fatigue. So, into the night-world of *Apparitions* (*VP*, p. 63) comes this demoralizing sensation:

> Tout à coup, dans la nuit, comme un brusque coup de pompe dans la poitrine, au cœur, mais ce n'est pas le coup de pompe qui donne, c'est celui qui retire, qui retire, vous laissant au bord de l'évanouissement, au bord de l'horreur sans sujet, au bord du 'plus rien'.

In many of the poet's visions, the body runs riot and has a frightening independence. With no sense of hierarchy or coordination, a tongue tears itself from a human mouth and rejoins the watery world of fish, an arm waves goodbye and disappears into the distance, bumping clumsily into things on its way. The narrator's leg has grown out of a hangar, cumbersome beyond measure yet infinitely fragile, and must be dragged back now that the work-bell has sounded before the workmen come stumbling in and dropping their tools on it. The head is especially prone to

disproportion. Lolling hydrocephalic heads held by a thread on
to a Belsen body (reminiscent of Laforgue's morbid drawings)
make frequent visitations. Alternatively, it is a tiny pin-head of
a head desperate to hold together an enormous rambling body,
like the captain of a crippled ship trying to prevent a flotilla of
rafts from deserting. Sometimes the poet has a hundred heads
pointing ahead of him like sticks to show the way, or finds himself
caught in a twirling cog-system of ratcheted heads, or cuts off
his head to improve his own equilibrium. Images of deformity
and mutilation are common: heaps of contorted limbs, pancake-
women struggling for shape, fœtuses interfered with in the womb
and doomed to be malformed. These overflow almost indis-
tinguishably into the themes of degenerate nature, creative
impotence and paralysis. The would-be creator rears 'un tout
petit cheval' (*Pl*, pp. 17–18), a poignant misshapen dwarf which
will never take its place in the world; he tries to teach a statue
to walk, rehearsing step after step in front of it, but there is
always something missing and the longed-for departure never
takes place. The same impotence emasculates words as they seek
to impinge on reality: as he preaches from a platform, it collapses
and he is dragged from the water as a fish and sold by the pound;
he preaches again but finds himself in a stew-pot where the noise
makes him drowsy and saps his will; and all that is left, when the
attempt to give voice has been consistently thwarted by the tur-
bulence and unpredictability of events, is to make 'un geste vague'
as a last futile act of relief (*Pl*, p. 22). In the 'Atelier de démolition'
(*VP*, pp. 72–3), his muscles are systematically extracted by
manikins with mallets and punches; he is determined to say
something before it is too late but 'Je ne trouve rien à leur dire.
Exactement rien. Sous les coups qui continuent, je m'enfonce
dans une paralysie d'adieu'.

A final place should be given to Michaux's monsters and the
profusion of animal life in his visions. 'Il fut bientôt évident (dès
mon adolescence) que j'étais né pour vivre parmi les monstres'
(*EE*, p. 99), he writes, and 'c'était soudée à la mienne, la vie des
monstres' (*EE*, p. 102). Men-snakes which drop from wardrobes,
giant larvae, a headless being climbing a pole with one gelatinous
leg, a monstrous hermaphrodite with huge thighs and moist
zones capable of undermining the stoutest self-respect, pour in
through the gaps where hierarchies have collapsed. The animal

substratum in human nature is no longer held in subordination. The poet can no longer say: 'Aussi surveillons-nous tous les mouvements suspects du monde animal (y ayant trop de parents permanents pour y être indifférents)' (*FV*, p. 111). Illness is the most effective means of release. A nightmarish cortège of 'animaux fantastiques' (*Pl*, pp. 55–63), changing shapes, exchanging parts, surges endlessly through the theatre of the feverish mind: beasts with trunks which probe the umbilicus, bitches with blue leprous wombs, creatures cocking their leg to relieve themselves and showing a green cynical eye, animals whose looks interrogate so implacably that they must be 'émissaires du Juge', a weasel with a fractured skull revealing a bleeding brain and a metal toothed wheel, prehistoric monsters and extinct species rising from the mud, described elsewhere as 'la boue, terreur de nos ancêtres, signe prédécesseur des grands cataclysmes' (*FV*, p. 217). Born in the folds of hidden anxieties and obsessions, 'Ils tombent, ils vous assaillent, ils n'ont de centre qu'en vous'.

Among the many movements of Michaux's inner world, one partnership has particular importance: that between 'attractions malsaines' and 'envies impossibles' (*FV*, p. 14). It is largely within this duality that the contours of dream and nightmare are drawn. Each grotesque or awesome vision, it seems, has its counterpart in another direction. So, the dreamer whose arm goes plunging with a frantic blood-lust among internal organs and spongy bits of lung can say: 'Dans le fond ce que j'aimerais, c'est de trouver de la rosée, très douce, bien apaisante' (*LNR*, p. 11) and speak of a love-dream forced by some involuntary perversity to express itself as aggression: 'Tel partit pour un baiser qui rapporta une tête' (*LNR*, p. 12). But sometimes ideal impulses or aspirations find their expression unimpeded. Michaux writes:

Il est pourtant quelques beaux rêves, qui correspondent à l'aura du mot 'rêve', à beauté, étendue, grandeur, dépassement, et qui une fois racontés font rêver avec nostalgie ceux qui les ont eus, et avec jalousie ceux qui n'en ont jamais eu de pareils. (*FF*, p. 185)

Instead of solitude and personal impotence, there is the vision, reminiscent of Rimbaud's 'Villes', in which 'tout respire la générosité des forces des éléments et de la race humaine au travail' (*LNR*, pp. 22–3): the poet, drawn into a joyous collective dynamism where hammers ring in unison and his room assumes a festive air, finds a kind of redemption in a primeval social identity 'si dense et extraordinaire qu'on perd de vue ses petites fins personnelles'. Instead of fatigue, bodily encumbrance and paralysis, he sees himself endowed with the utmost speed and spontaneity of movement. As the world's perfect diver, totally at one with a miraculous current which eliminates all self-consciousness and deliberate effort, he can boast: 'Je plonge comme le sang coule dans mes veines. Oh! glissement dans l'eau!' (*LNR*, p. 21). Just as Baudelaire, in his 'Elevation', celebrates an unadulterated ethereal freedom unknown in those more ambiguous poems where 'l'horreur de la vie et l'extase de la vie'[14] intermingle, so Michaux escapes from constriction, degradation and human competition as he skates alone with unimaginable facility along the pure vein of a frozen river.

Such images, however, serve only to re-emphasize the general ambivalence of this visionary world. Movement can be exhilaration and speed or vertigo and the torment of everlasting change. Space can be dilation, purification and redemption or the ravaging suction of a terrible vacuum. Matter and solidity may be a safe retreat after a venture into the void or a grotesque prison and persecutor. Alienation from his 'larves et fantômes fidèles' (*Ec*, p. 76) can be as terrifying as their proximity. A dream-sensation can change its nature in a flash and become its own opposite. Michaux's inner space is all tensions: just as in Apollinaire's 'La Chanson du mal-aimé' an ideal of 'corps blancs des amoureuses' reigns among the constellations over the turmoil of images of blood and fire, so in 'La Nuit remue' the bleeding eiderdown and dead body engender the dream of an 'Etoile de corps blancs, qui toujours rayonne, rayonne...' (*LNR*, p. 7); and as the strange genetic drop falls from the ceiling to form a misshapen woman, a nostalgia is born for the grace which might have been: 'Longues étaient ses jambes, longues. Elle eût fait une danseuse' (*LNR*, p. 9).

TRAVEL

'Moi j'aime les issues' (*LNR*, p. 69): Michaux might have adopted as his own the motto of Gide's Protos, 'passer outre'. The major preoccupation of his life has been to step beyond himself, beyond his situation at any given moment, beyond any accomplishment which threatens to content him and become a status quo. In his dream-encounter with the owner of the lock-eating animal which eats its way through to room after room he senses, despite a secret unity, that their interests are not quite compatible: 'je lui dis que moi ce que je préférais dans la vie, était de sortir' (*Pl*, p. 21). The sight of motorbikes speeding away to the horizon in a matter of seconds and then lingering interminably there as if loath to disappear leaves nostalgic onlookers 'recueillis aux fenêtres, aux fenêtres, aux fenêtres aux grands horizons' (*Pl*, p. 25). Analysing the rôle of trains in his dreams, the author writes:

Il est vrai, les trains pour moi ont dû être importants, me sauvant de l'environnement, des lieux et des situations détestables où je me trouvais. Ils ont d'abord été liés aux fugues, à la fuite, au soulagement de la fuite, à l'aventure, aux exaltants quoique médiocres débuts de mon moi en quête d'inconnu. (*FF*, pp. 54–5)

His numerous extensive journeys from 1929 onwards he describes as aggressive 'voyages d'expatriation' (Bréchon, p. 21), undertaken to break with his heredity, nationality and acquired culture. Few poets have been as addicted to movement and displacement as Michaux. In the poem-epitaph 'Qu'il repose en révolte' he sees his ultimate image 'Dans la route qui obsède... dans le voyageur que l'espace ronge' (*VP*, p. 117); and of the character Plume it is said, 'il voyage, il voyage continuellement' (*Pl*, p. 143).[15]

It is impossible to assess the many factors which may have played in Michaux's decision to set off in the last days of 1927 on a year's journey to the Amazon. Perhaps his aim was to re-open that window to which he refers when, in 1921, ships were laid up all over the world and he was forced to give up his brief seafaring life: 'La grande fenêtre se referme. Il doit se détourner de la mer' (Bréchon, p. 19). Perhaps he wished to break the circle of self-enclosure, his sterile *anti-vie*. Perhaps he needed to clear himself, if only temporarily, of the discordant clutter of *qui-je-fus* or exorcize by transplantation some of the more obsessive and frustrating 'larves et fantômes fidèles' of his inner universe. Perhaps the prison of Paris itself, with its false problems and hard-won existence, had become stifling. Whatever the most compelling reason, there is evidence of two years' anticipation of this journey, two years of blockage and immobility which make the final departure almost inconceivable: 'Deux ans, une sorte de constipation et maintenant, c'est pour mardi matin' (*Ec*, p. 11). There is evidence, too, of a degree of romanticism, an idealization which makes reminders of reality and his own self seem an impurity:

Je suis soumis toute la journée à une sorte de projection à distance. On cherche mon regard. Quel effort il me faut pour revenir à moi, et combien 'impur' ce retour, comme quand on cède à une image de sexe dans la prière. (*Ec*, p. 11)

Yet *Ecuador* (1929) turns out to be the ironic antithesis of exoticism, a travel-journal of the absurd. The anticipated relief from constipation becomes nothing but an aimless evacuation. Words, consigning the virtual to paper as drab fact and promise as still-born achievement, are an immediate death-process: 'Je n'ai écrit que ce peu qui précède et déjà je tue ce voyage. Je le croyais si grand. Non, il fera des pages, c'est tout, son urine quotidienne' (*Ec*, p. 11). The journey, as imagined, never materializes. Stranded among senseless fragments, irrelevances and non-events, the narrator repeats these words like a refrain: 'Et ce voyage, mais où est-il ce voyage?' (*Ec*, p. 17). There is nothing to feed the Romantic imagination. Gone are Baudelairean boats bathed in the scents of tamarisk trees, slipping through surfaces of gold and shot silk, opening their arms to embrace the sky or sinking replete into the warmth of the evening air. In their place is the *Boskoop*: 'avec les mâts de charge levés, ses poulies, ses cordages sales, cette superstructure d'insecte et puis l'intestin de sa quille, un salmis sans nom. Pouah!' (*Ec*, p. 27). A group of Indians threads its way gravely through a town, perhaps in some secret ritual or towards an exotic goal. But no, the hardly formulated speculation fizzles out in pointlessness and banality:

Où va-t-il ce pèlerinage voûté?
Il se croise et s'entrecroise et monte; rien de plus: c'est la vie quotidienne. (*Ec*, p. 34)

The lack of correspondence between idea and fact, expectation and event is so absolute that language, like a cold motor, cannot even start and only coughs in the void. The end-product of a 15,000 foot climb to the volcanic crater of the Atacatzho is nothing but:

Ah! Ah!
Cratère?   ah!
On s'attendait à un peu plus de sérieux...
Ah! ...

(*Ec*, p. 121)

At an early stage of the journey, the traveller's mind is made up: 'Non, je l'ai déjà dit ailleurs. Cette terre est rincée de son exotisme...nous n'en pouvons plus de rester sur cette écorce' (*Ec*, pp. 36–7).

Ecuador is primarily the record of an absurd confrontation with reality. There are no *nourritures terrestres*. There is no prospect of communion. Camus writes:

Cette épaisseur et cette étrangeté du monde, c'est l'absurde... s'apercevoir que le monde est 'épais', entrevoir à quel point une pierre est étrangère, nous est irréductible, avec quelle intensité la nature, un paysage peut nous nier.[16]

Meeting for the first time the volcanic earth of the Andes plateaux, Michaux comments (in sealed, unyielding phrases) on its inhospitality, its introversion, its contempt:

Le sol est noir et sans accueil.
Un sol venu du dedans.
Il ne s'intéresse pas aux plantes.
(*Ec*, p. 35)

The boggy surface of the tropical forest of the Napo is no better, showing the same indifference to human interests and expectations: 'Le sol mou s'en fout, ne dit ni oui ni non' (*Ec*, p. 136). The landscape rejects the traveller and leaves him wondering what is his place there, if any. The rare scene of which he can say: 'Cela me plaît et entre en moi' (*Ec*, p. 95) serves only to confirm the extent to which reality remains foreign, unassimilable. Virtually nothing filters through to ferment a relationship. He and the crust of the phenomenal world stand there in senseless opposition. 'Ici comme partout, 999.999 spectacles mal foutus sur 1.000.000 et que je ne sais comment prendre', writes the disenchanted diarist, 'Non, je ne peux accepter. Il faut que je m'en aille plus loin' (*Ec*, pp. 47–8). The local people stiffen the sense of sterility. As they wend their way in their empty mock-procession, the Indians are hunched, stunted, unadventurous figures: 'Trapus, brachycéphales, à petits pas' (*Ec*, p. 34). Others, passing among the houses, are seen as 'Une lente circulation de caillots de sang' (*Ec*, p. 36). They are a dwarf people without resonance or radiation, devoid of spiritual attainment. In mocking answer to a friend who writes that he has seen wax models of Equatorial Indians in the Berlin museum and enthuses: 'Quelle poésie ils contiennent!', Michaux replies: 'Un Indien, un homme quoi! Un homme comme les autres, prudent, sans départs, qui n'arrive à rien, qui ne cherche pas, l'homme "comme ça" '. And he concludes: 'Une fois pour toutes, voici: Les hommes qui n'aident pas à mon perfectionnement: Zéro' (*Ec*, pp.102–3).

The journey simply throws him back on his own self-awareness. It touches his obsessions without alleviating them. Images of imprisonment, claustrophobia, physical weakness, victimization, impotence, monstrous animal persecutors and personal annihilation hedge his route. The first sight of the Andes brings on a sensation close to despair: 'L'horizon d'abord disparaît' (*Ec*, p. 34) and the capital city of Quito is 'l'étouffement même' (*Ec*, p. 86). The gluey vegetal masses of the jungle floor pull one off balance and into an infinity of miniature *gouffres*; the tropical climate 'vous suce en douce, vous pompe à blanc' (*Ec*, p. 178), gradually turning a person into an absence. The natural environment around Quito has 'un *je veux, je ne peux* d'arbustes, de taillis qui n'arrive qu'à gêner' (*Ec*, p. 111). Vampire spiders, hacked with machetes, drop from the walls in sticky fragments and bleeding abdominal sections; destructive little filiform creatures penetrate you in the water; carnivorous fish reduce a body to nothing in a few minutes, explaining why a floating corpse is never found in the Amazon. So, when the author suggests to himself one day that he might do a colour-painting of what he has seen, his own inner phantoms write themselves on to the canvas, appropriating the picture and showing the irrelevance of the Equator or any other part of the globe to the essential *problème d'être*: 'Mais le moi de moi n'a pas voulu et sur la toile sont apparues mes larves et fantômes fidèles, qui ne sont de nulle part, ne connaissent rien de l'Equateur, ne se laisseraient pas faire' (*Ec*, p. 76). A year's venture passes like a useless mirage, leaving his own life and purpose unresolved. The traveller's conclusion, which clears the way for 'journeys' of another kind, could almost have been predicted from the outset:

Maintenant ma conviction est faite. Ce voyage est une gaffe. Le voyage ne rend pas tant large que mondain, 'au courant'...On trouve aussi bien sa vérité en regardant 48 heures une quelconque tapisserie de mur. (*Ec*, p. 126)

But despite the sense of futility and self-disgust implicit in the words: 'Déjà écrire d'imagination était médiocre, mais écrire à propos d'un spectacle extérieur!' (*Ec*. p. 76), this is not to be Michaux's only travel-account. *Un Barbare en Asie* (1933) renews his dealings with the genre. Moreover, the author's retrospective comments on his wide-ranging travels through the Far East in 1930–1 show clearly that these were no drab continuation of the South American experience. The opening words of *Un Barbare en Asie* provide an important key: 'Aux Indes, rien à voir, tout à interpréter' (*BA*, p. 11). Whereas Ecuador was a meaningless crust, hiding and reflecting nothing, here everything suggests a further dimension. External reality, no longer sullenly self-enclosed and self-sufficient, is transfused by forces or meanings beyond itself and becomes a network of signs and provocations. This is a text, therefore, more concerned with the implicit or potential than the real. Behind the diversity of external scenes and spectacles, Michaux is pursuing, as if in a series of rapid *parcours*, a contact with the spirit, the underlying rhythms and *raison d'être* of the peoples and places concerned. (One thinks of A.'s early reading, where individual words themselves were only of secondary importance to a communion with some nebulous essence, some fleeting communication, sensed behind the surface.) But this does not prevent *Un Barbare en Asie* from being a work of colourful, animated reporting. Whether his focus fixes on oriental religion, culture, art or language, on the picturesque or the portentous, street-scenes or spiritual secrets, on the Calcutta crowd, the Tamil language, the *Rig Veda*, the virginal architecture of the Taj Mahal, a Himalayan railway, Chinese music, Eastern attitudes to love and death, the spirit of the willow, or the *Wayang Koelit* (shadow theatre) of Java and Bali, Michaux's style is pliable, effervescent and inventive, alive with surprising images, crisp turns of phrase, dramatic ellipses, variable sentence-structures, quaint and humorous asides—all indicative of that 'joie de revivre' of which he speaks and the 'abondance des choses nouvelles' (*BA*, p. 95). It is an eager, acquisitive style, reflecting a year of diverse plundering through a variety of countries and

3—HM * *

the rapid consigning to his mental honeycomb of the savours of that *butinage*.

The prime attraction of the Hindu people, seen as 'le peuple de l'Absolu, le peuple radicalement religieux' (*BA*, p. 25), is that they themselves are largely indifferent to the face of the visible world. In this, Michaux suggests (in an amusing piece with a sly irony showing that, even in admiration, he loses nothing of his critical detachment), the ruminant, imperturbable sacred cow is their appropriate symbol: 'Visiblement, elle ne cherche pas d'explication, ni de vérité dans le monde extérieur. *Maya* tout cela. Maya, ce monde. Ça ne compte pas' (*BA*, p. 16). Their thought, in contrast to the self-contained circuits of the intellect so common to Western philosophy, is not idly severed from essential universal forces: 'Ce ne sont pas des pensées, pour penser, ce sont des pensées pour participer à l'Etre, à BRAHMA' (*BA*, p. 21). Remarks in the poet's latest writings on the effects of drugs emphasize the extent to which Hinduism has continued to feed his own explorations. The Hindu, he says, is inclined to create divinity from all things and gives himself to a boundless urge towards the divine, just as in the Upanishads or great epic texts like the Mahabharata one feels that same 'entraînement à l'impossible où le sacré force les barrières de la vie' (*MM*, p. 191). Michaux highlights the differences between Hinduism and Christianity. Whereas Christianity (with its *De profundis clamavi ad te, Domine*, its Gothic cathedrals which dwarf the faithful and its cries for pity, 'Kyrie Eleison') impresses the quality of humility and the depths of man's degradation and weakness, Hindu religion releases man's awareness of his own strength and his right to possess the gods by force: 'Celui qui prie bien fait tomber des pierres, parfume les eaux. Il *force* Dieu. Une prière est un rapt. Il y faut une bonne tactique' (*BA*, p. 26). One has the unique prospect of the reconciliation of universal Spirit and self-possession, absorption into the Everything and self-determination, ecstasy and technique: a model of 'Sérénité dans la puissance' which would seem to give an answer to the dilemma voiced by Rimbaud: 'Je veux la liberté dans le salut: comment la poursuivre?'[17] Asking why the Hindu religion is probably that most likely to be adopted by present and future minds, Michaux replies: 'Surtout, parce qu'elle est *prométhéenne*. Elle part de l'homme conquérant des forces cachées' (*MM*, p. 193).

In more general terms, India offers the traveller a rich illustration of the cult of mental control. For the person who has complained: 'J'ai rarement rencontré dans ma vie des gens qui avaient besoin comme moi d'être regonflés à chaque instant' (*LNR*, p. 103), the appeal of a people whom he can describe as

Attentifs et renforcés...lents, contrôlés et gonflés...
Concentrés, ne se livrant à la rue et au torrent de l'existence que rétifs, bordés intérieurement, engaînés et survoltés (*BA*, p. 15)

is obvious. For the sceptic who has said: 'Une fois pour toutes, voici: Les hommes qui n'aident pas à mon perfectionnement: Zéro' (*Ec*, pp. 102–3), there are certainly points to be scored for those who, 'sans que ça soit clair, vous donnent l'impression d'intervenir quelque part en soi, comme vous ne le pourriez pas' (*BA*, p. 17). And for the man whose thoughts have been chronically dispersed or reduced to nothing by a variety of pernicious internal forces, the prospect of a supremely efficacious magic thought acting directly on the self and on the phenomenal world must hold a special attraction.

The influence of China is less easy to determine. Michaux himself has said that it had a delayed-action effect and deserved longer meditation than his excessively hasty journey gave it. Perhaps it proposed above all a secret of conquest by means of patience and meticulous technique ('Gouvernez l'empire comme vous cuiriez un petit poisson' is the quotation from Lao Tzu placed as an epigraph to the whole of *Un Barbare en Asie*); or an art of unobtrusiveness and self-effacement, both on a social level and on the more mystical plane suggested by Taoism; or the achievement of a delicate equilibrium and harmony which, for the Chinese, constitutes a sort of paradise on earth. Perhaps, on the other hand, its artistic forms were the deepest revelation: its pacific cathartic music; its weightless painting dealing only in suggestions of movement and line; its evasive poetry which never once stumbles on anything as cumbersome as an idea (in the Western sense of the word); its theatre of dynamic signs; its traditional attachment to the willow with its affective play of *frissons*. However complex or nebulous the appeal, there is little doubt that China and the experience of the Far East were to trace deep routes in Michaux's sensitivity and stimulate his future work in innumerable hidden ways.

Yet, perhaps surprisingly, the conclusion of *Un Barbare en Asie*
reinforces that of *Ecuador*. There is the implication that this, too,
is a wasted journey: 'Après avoir parlé de la mentalité de certains
peuples, on se demande vraiment si ça en valait la peine, si on
n'aurait pas mieux occupé son temps d'une autre façon' (*BA*,
pp. 212–13). To talk of Malays, Javanese, Balinese and so on,
married and intermingled with Bataks, Dayaks, Chinese, Arabs
etc. etc. is only to realize what a bottomless, heterogeneous world
it is and how empty any general comment on it becomes. One
country's 'truth', moreover, is no more valid or reliable than
another's. And in any case: 'Qu'est-ce qu'une civilisation? Une
impasse' (*BA*, p. 237). Throughout the text runs an implicit
message of self-containment: the Calcutta crowd is a 'Foule
franche qui se baigne en elle-même, ou plutôt chacun en soi'
(*BA*, p. 14); they are a race of *étrangers*, 'Immobiles et n'attendant
rien de personne' (*BA*, p. 16); the pilgrims by the Ganges at
Benares are hermetically sealed from each other, 'chacun pour
soi attentif à son salut' (*BA*, p. 66); and, according to the law
that 'Moins quelqu'un est abordable, plus il a de vie intérieure'
(*BA*, p. 127), there can be no communication with the most
spiritually involved. The author is finally thrown back on the
resources of his own interior just as surely as in *Ecuador*:

> Ainsi quand on se retire en soi, fuyant le monde, et qu'on arrive à
> supprimer cette énorme superstructure et ce multiple débat, on arrive à
> une paix, à un plan tellement inouï qu'on pourrait se demander si ce
> n'est pas cela le 'surnaturel'. (*BA*, p. 237)

Having begun with Lao Tzu, he ends with the words of the
dying Buddha:

> A l'avenir, soyez votre propre lumière, votre propre refuge.
> Ne cherchez pas d'autre refuge.
> N'allez en quête de refuge qu'auprès de vous-même.
> Ne vous occupez pas des façons de penser des autres.
> Tenez-vous bien dans votre île à vous.
> COLLES A LA CONTEMPLATION.

As a Surrealist letter says: 'L'Orient est partout…En Europe
même, qui peut dire où n'est pas l'Orient? Dans la rue, l'homme
que vous croisez le porte en lui: l'Orient est dans sa conscience'.[18]

POETIC MAGIC

Already in *Ecuador* there was a tendency for Michaux to be elsewhere. 'Je ne suis plus à Quito, je suis dans la lecture' (*Ec*, p. 43), he writes. When the port of Iquitos becomes unbearable, he temporarily changes his proportions, disengages from reality and finds himself projected afar, safely buffered in a world of fiction:

> J'aurais voulu passer inaperçu; je me faisais tout petit et j'arrivais à Paris, où je me cachais dans les livres.
> Mais bientôt je me réveillais avec encore tout le Brésil à traverser. (*Ec*, p. 175)

In an essay in *Passages* he describes how, even from childhood, he was aware that he was alive with inner movements (all potential journeys) which pressed upon his vision: 'Des mouvements dont, en fait, on ne voyait pas trace en mon attitude et dont on n'aurait pu avoir le soupçon, sauf par un certain air d'absence et de savoir m'abstraire' (*Pass*, p. 200). Michaux's ability to absent himself is given fluency by the fact that so-called reality never appears to be quite real. One piece in *Ecuador* is called 'Mirage d'une ville indienne' (*Ec*, p. 36); and observations such as 'une ville nouvelle, on n'arrive pas tout à fait à y croire', 'Quito ne me semble pas encore tout à fait réel' or 'toute contrée étrangère paraît un peu mascarade' (*Ec*, pp. 39–40) are frequent. Throughout his work there is an easy osmosis between fact and fiction, physical and mental vision: 'Penser, vivre, mer peu distincte' (*Pl*, p. 88). On the one hand, a whole year's contact with the Amazon disappears as if it had never existed:

> Voyant une grosse année réduite à si peu de pages, l'auteur est ému. Sûrement il s'est passé encore bien d'autres choses.
> Le voilà qui cherche. Mais il ne rencontre que brouillards... (*Ec*, p. 181)

or, as in the case of Japan, a country may have no stable reality but simply lose or acquire it, be done and undone, according to a mental perspective: 'Tandis que beaucoup de pays qu'on a aimés, deviennent à mesure qu'on s'en éloigne, presque ridicules ou inconsistants, le Japon que j'ai nettement détesté, me devient presque cher' (*BA*, p. 206). In a footnote to an analysis of Indian hemp, Michaux says categorically that his real 'souvenirs de voyage...sont si flous et vagues, si difficiles à retrouver, si extrême- ment atténués que, panier percé, il ne me reste d'autres ressources que de me remettre à voyager'. On the other hand, a mental spectacle may be 'Si vrai en un mot qu'on s'en souviendra comme d'un endroit unique où l'on s'est trouvé véritablement' (*CG*, p. 124). One of the remarkable features of dream, he notes, is its emphatic and convincing *mise en scène*: one is not aware of the images as signs crossing the mind but as 'spectacles du dehors auxquels on assiste réellement' (*FF*, p. 172). (Rimbaud has said, 'j'assiste à l'éclosion de ma pensée: je la regarde, je l'écoute: je lance le coup d'archet: la symphonie fait son remuement dans les profondeurs, ou vient d'un bond sur la scène'.[19]) So many of Michaux's obsessions leap out of the mind and project themselves spontaneously on to a wall or screen or into the web of a visible tapestry: in the case of his 'animaux fantastiques', 'ils sortent des tapisseries les plus simples, grimaçant à la moindre courbe, profitant d'une ligne verticale pour s'élancer' (*Pl*, p. 55). There are innumerable forms of actual physical life, moreover, which appear stranger than fiction and might easily have stepped out of the imagination: strange hybrids like the *Chuchora machacu* of the Amazon, an insect with a hippopotamus-like head and tiny eyes perched at the back, or the *Autennarius hipsidus* of the Madras aquarium, with its horseshoe chin and yellow flannel-waistcoat skin—unprecedented living creatures all 'surgis de l'inconnu' (*BA*, p. 95).

It is in part this unclear dividing-line which enables Michaux to tamper so easily with reality, to dispense with the facts and embroider at will. He shows himself intrigued in China by the idea of ideography: the way in which children in their games take a sign to symbolize an idea (two uneven bits of wood become a boat and a gangway, a chance play of light and shade on the ground becomes a river-bank) and then, perfectly at one with their signs, elaborate a play of movement and drama. One can see a link here with what is to become an important characteristic of the poet's own art: an art in which signs, far more malleable and versatile, act in place of reality or, viewed in another way, an art in which aspects of reality are turned from their natural place and function and re-employed to serve the sign. Michaux has no respect for reality as a value in its own right. Confronted with the sterility of Ecuador, he feels the need to intervene and correct the real: 'Aucune contrée ne me plaît: voilà le voyageur que je suis...*Si je pouvais donner du relief à une province...*' (*Ec*, p. 43). Speaking of his attachment to the possibilities of day-dreams or waking dreams, he refers to himself as 'celui qui ne trouve pas que ça vaille la peine de s'éveiller complètement et de voir ce monde complètement dans son concret, son limité, son fermé, son déterminé' (*FF*, p. 82). In a piece from *Ecuador*, important in that it prefigures the poet's famous imaginary countries of the years 1936–46 and shows the value of the poetic imagination not only as an agent of wish fulfilment but as a shock absorber and a reliever of tension, he writes:

> Une habitude très mienne. Voici les circonstances: c'est quand je suis étendu et que néanmoins le sommeil ne vient pas. Alors je me comble. Je me donne en esprit tout ce qu'il me plaît d'obtenir. Partant de faits personnels toujours réels et d'une ligne si plausible, j'arrive doucement à me faire sacrer roi de plusieurs pays, ou quelque chose de ce genre. Cette habitude est aussi vieille que ma mémoire, et je ne reste pas plusieurs jours sans me donner cette satisfaction. C'est pourquoi je sors du lit avec une grande paix. S'il arrive que le temps m'ait fait défaut pour cela, je grelotte dans la journée, l'air et les paroles d'autrui me sont aigus. (*Ec*, p. 49)

It becomes clear that, after *Un Barbare en Asie*, Michaux finds no further purpose in recording external journeys or reproducing known peoples. Even while in the East, he is aware that the physical details, the observable facts, are largely irrelevant: 'C'est la façon, le style et non les faits qui comptent' (*BA*, p. 216); and it is on the basis of such intangible styles, accents or rhythms that he is to fashion his own half-real, half-imaginary races in the world of *Ailleurs*. While in Bali, he can see the point of trying to sculpture a demon—just as in painting, if he could bring himself to launch any school ending in *-ism*, it would be what he calls 'le FANTOMISME' (*Pass*, p. 93)—but he feels only the futility of depicting real men and women. Accordingly, his own efforts in creating the populations of 'Grande Garabagne' or 'Poddema' will be governed, not by some mimetic instinct, but by 'la soif de transformer, de refaire, de dépasser...d'ajouter aux millions de "possibles"' (*Aill*, Préface). As far as journeys in the real world are concerned, his conclusion comes close to that of Des Esseintes who, tempted to go chasing his ideal in England when he has already been disillusioned by Holland, says: 'A quoi bon bouger, quand on peut voyager si magnifiquement sur une chaise?'[20] Plume himself, tossed across the face of the globe to feel only the shocks of his incompatibility with reality, has the premonition of a quieter, more personal kind of travel: 'Il aime mieux voyager avec modestie. Tant que ce sera possible, il le fera' (*Pl*, p. 141). It is in this way that, like Michaux's *l'insoumis*, 'Sans remuer un doigt, il aura été un grand aventurier' (*Pl*, p. 70). The poet's new journeys will take place essentially 'dans la campagne immense de l'être intérieur' (*Pl*, p. 131), in vast stretches of mental hinter-land, far more real than the charted physical world, from which he returns 'comme revenu de voyage avec un passé plein de choses' (*GE*, p. 46): 'Il ne s'est pourtant passé que des pensées, et pendant peu de temps, mais des pensées comme des lieux, des salles, des places où j'aurais été'. The title-piece of the collection *Liberté d'Action* (1945), though written after the creation of two of the three great countries, Grande Garabagne, the Pays de la Magie and Poddema, leads one to the very door of Michaux's imaginary lands:

Je ne voyage plus. Pourquoi que ça m'intéresserait les voyages?
Ce n'est pas ça. Ce n'est jamais ça.
Je peux l'arranger moi-même leur pays.
De la façon qu'ils s'y prennent, il y a toujours trop de choses qui ne portent pas.
Ils se sont donné du mal inutilement, ces New-Yorkais avec leurs gratteciels, si faciles à survoler, ces Chinois avec leurs pagodes et leur civilisation de derrière les fagots. Moi, je mets la Chine dans ma cour. Je suis plus à l'aise pour l'observer. (*VP*, pp. 23–4)

It is an important aspect of the poet's 'magic' that he himself, free from the uncomfortable proximity and coercions of reality, should be able to arrange and re-arrange it at will and enjoy a measure of detachment and *disponibilité*. He writes: 'Je veux plutôt un monde potentiel que réel. Je veux en disposer, plutôt que de l'avoir, "avoir" étant toujours "avoir partie liée avec" ' (*FF*, p. 220). His private countries are yet another proof of his lack of permanent solidarity with life.

Ailleurs (1948) contains three works: *Voyage en Grande Garabagne* (1936), *Au Pays de la Magie* (1941)[21] and *Ici Poddema* (1946). The countries described here belong to strange intermediary zones, situated between the familiar and the foreign, the freakish and the frightening, the delicate and the disquieting. Their fascination stems partly from the fact that they defy definition. Like surreal mirrors, they give glints of a recognizable image and then cloud over, offer semblances of order and then recoil into obscurity. Their impact is all the more emphatic in that the narrator maintains throughout the cool, logical style of the social anthropologist, interested tourist or scientific observer, setting up a fertile, sometimes ironic, tension between fact and fantasy, unperturbed notations and inexplicable events, conscientious accuracy and patent ignorance. One arrives in these lands without forewarning or explanation, to be plunged among peoples and spectacles without precedent in an atmosphere of mystery and malaise. In Grande Garabagne one becomes the forced onlooker to the ritual battle of the Hacs, in which two half-naked men, shod in heavy wooden clogs, slowly and deliberately kick each other to death on a platform while the surrounding public sets up an eerie concert of low groans: 'Râles de passions complexes, ces plaintes inhumaines s'élevaient comme d'immenses tentures autour de ce combat' (*Aill*, p. 12). One meets the subtle temperament of the Emanglons, described cryptically as 'sans antennes, mais au fond mouvant': moved to tears by the trembling of a leaf or a falling speck of dust which becomes a total *bouleversement*, drawn by 'une espèce de dégel intérieur accompagné de frissons' (*Aill*, p. 37) into a mysterious group catharsis, favouring faint muted forms of music which seem to be played through a mattress. One observes the curious foot-dance of the Orbu women; the 'black puddings' growing under the skin of the Nans; the terrible diarrhoea of the Ourgouilles. One cannot quite grasp the secret unity of these eccentric 'tribes', individually or collectively, nor ascertain their degree of humanity or inhumanity. But they send uncomfortable probes deep into human nature, hold a critical mirror up to our strengths and weaknesses, pretensions and aberrations, and above all propose a challenging revaluation of the human species as a whole and its very definition. *Au Pays de la Magie* is a work of a different flavour. It is not a pageant of multiple tribes, customs and social mores, nor does it concern itself with the depiction of such basic, though complex, instinctive and emotional impulses as those found in *Voyage en Grande Garabagne*. It focuses on a single people, the Mages, and on the more ethereal forces which surround them,

animate them and constitute the enigmatic fabric of their everyday life. And whereas the Emanglons were 'sans antennes', the
Mages are very definitely '*avec* antennes'. As birds squawk and
scrape inside cages but remain totally invisible, as water stands
there holding itself together when its carafe has broken, as
wrongdoers have their faces ripped off by occult intervention, or
as a dangerous luminous sleeve leaps about in the night air, one
comes alive to the unexplained play of absence and presence, the
magic potential, the innumerable telecommunications and
untapped energies which move in the space within and around
the human mind (or the human mind as it might be). *Ici Poddema*,
with its view of a more systematic futuristic social organization,
moves nearer to traditional utopian literature. One zone,
Poddema-Ama, has many features of a 'brave new world': the
specially prepared public 'loving-walls' of Langalore give ineffable relief from tensions; in the sphere of crime and punishment,
imminent anti-social acts are detected before they can find
expression; different scales of suffering ensure that the people
are educated in the art of true humanity. But a horrific reverse
side maintains the country's ambiguity. For in Poddema-Nara
one is faced with the mad flies, stunted boys and degenerate
domestic monkeys of Kannaverrina, a place-name evoking
cannibalism, cadavers, worms and vermin; with the women of
Narodi whose orifices pour blood in the act of love; and with the
inexhaustible stock of 'Poddemaïs au pot', men bred artificially
in the flesh pots, some trained up trellis-work, some with twenty
or thirty edible buttocks, others sold for their coveted blue
eyes.

Michaux calls his imaginary countries 'des sortes d'Etats-
tampons, afin de ne pas souffrir de la réalité' (*Pass*, pp. 153–4).
Just as Plume was a 'buffer-character' thrown up during a
journey to Turkey behind whom the poet himself retreated in
order to cushion the embarrassments of reality, so these lands,
with their intriguing characters, fanciful situations and distracting spectacles, stood between him and hostile people and
places, and enjoyed and suffered on his behalf. In a moment of
considerable pain in Ecuador Michaux started to smoke excessively, saying: 'Cela fait résistance et ouate' (*Ec*, p. 69), words
which apply perfectly to his 'buffer-states'. These imaginary
countries are also 'masked faces'. Describing the facial 'tatooing'

of certain South American Indians, who put patterns of coloured streaks on their faces when going to eat with friends and rub them off on returning home, Michaux comments that the Turks have observed the same truth, that the face itself, undisguised, is somehow indecent: 'Ça se jette au-dessus des vêtements et les regards en sortent comme des fous. Tout ce que la peau a de malsain et de bestial disparaît dès qu'il s'y trouve quelques traits ou grilles' (*Ec*, p. 187). Seen through a decorative lattice-work the face loses much of its brutality, becomes *d'esprit* and allows an otherwise impossible ease of communication. The poet's magic countries are similarly an artistic mask or grille ensuring comparatively painless exchanges between him and a reality which, in its raw state, in a denuded confrontation, could only repulse him. To some extent they stem from a spirit of play and constitute what he calls 'une nouvelle organisation ludique' (*Pass*, p. 181) of the world. They give the author the freedom to indulge in fantasy, 'l'indispensable fantaisie tellement à tort méprisée, signe de l'heureux excès de possibilités' (*CG*, p. 256). Writing elsewhere of all the extravagant impressions and associations which nudge the mind along 'le chemin du fantastique', he says that, whereas the sick mind has no means of rejecting them and the sane mind continually corrects and neutralizes them, the poet, on the contrary, 'essaie parfois leur fête' (*GE*, p. 44). This is all the more so when reality has caused conflict or friction: '...dès que la vie, les accidents de la vie, le déroulement de la vie m'a contrarié. Je n'ai plus de vie alors qu'imaginaire, qu' immédiate' (*FF*, p. 206). The vast landscapes of Grande Garabagne, the Pays de la Magie and Poddema are in a sense 'paysages d'accompagnement' (*Pass*, p. 46): scenes and visions more attuned to his own mental requirements than those of the real world. At the same time one could look upon them, not only as an artistic buffer, a screen or a fanciful extension of physical reality, but as a controlled, playful reorganization of his own lurking obsessions. In this way his elaborate waking dreams act as an antidote to uncomfortable night-dreams:

Peut-être est-ce encore plus contre mes rêves de nuit que contre ma vie, que je faisais mes dynamiques rêves de jour, rêveries que je savais rendre fascinantes, exaltantes.

Après les rêveries, plus besoin de rêves.

Nuits calmes, profondes. (*FF*, p. 41)

But one should not dismiss this *ailleurs* as an exercise in mere escapism. For together with the obvious compensatory images moves a <u>mass of rebellious and inexplicable ma</u>tter; and while holding reality at bay the buffer-states never cease to register its shocks and vibrations, thus justifying the poet's insistence when he says: 'Je vous le dis, je vous le dis, vraiment là où je suis, je connais aussi la vie' (*Pl*, p. 51). However imaginative and curious they may be, they are not remote private outposts. They are intermediaries, committed in an anxious balance of power and reflecting many of its vital stresses.

The foreign countries are only one manifestation, however, of what Michaux calls his 'appuis secrets' (*FV*, p. 12). In his semi-<u>philosophical maxims, his 'Tranches de savoir</u>' (*FV*, p. 76), he refers to those who fight with visible arms and will one day be mocked as they stand empty-handed. He, by contrast, has developed poetry as an armoury of *invisible* weapons and is rarely caught without resources. Perhaps his most basic procedure, built on the realization that external reality is nothing but an absurd skin with no particular validity, is 'intervention':

> Autrefois, j'avais trop le respect de la nature. Je me mettais devant les choses et les paysages et je les laissais faire.
> Fini, maintenant *j'interviendrai*. (*LNR*, p. 149)

Feeling the tedium of Honfleur, he applies will-power and meticulous method to introduce camels into the crowded market place, and then sits back as the spectacle runs its course according to a new logic, with the locals complaining about the stench and animals' hooves clanging all night on the metal bridges of the lock-gates. (One thinks of the example of Tulsi Das, quoted in *Un Barbare en Asie*, who by intense meditation conjured up an army of monkeys to pillage the town and liberate him.) In a piece entitled 'Magie', the poet traces the stages leading to the creation of a live frog: 'Plusieurs veulent obtenir des créations mentales en utilisant la méthode fakirique. C'est une erreur' (*LNR*, p. 141). His own method (calling to mind once more Lao Tzu's words that one should govern the empire as one would cook a little fish) is to implant the appropriate surrounding conditions with no undue haste, first sketching the picture in his mind, then painting in river-banks with an exact choice of greens, then waiting patiently for the river to arrive: after a while he will dip a stick over the bank and if it comes out wet it is only a matter of time before frogs will frolic in the vicinity. As before, in a way quite distinct from Surrealist 'automatism', a prolonged technical stage precedes a spontaneous one: the mental creation is slowly established to such a pitch that the fictional and the real, brought to the same density, can no longer be differentiated and slip automatically into a natural amalgam. There is no question of an hallucinatory *grand ensemble* surging ready-made into being: as a reception of vision rather than a willed creation, this would lack the necessary therapeutic self-control. On occasions a kind of 'intervention' does take place as if of its own accord. Michaux calls it 'projection'. One day in Honfleur it suddenly dawns on him that the spectacle he has been watching for hours is only an emanation of his mind; but his initial satisfaction that he has not after all spent the day uselessly gives way to anguish as the scene, not established by deliberate mental application, does not respond to mental application when he wishes to reverse the process and pull it back in, and stands there with a poisonous independence. Often the poet's interventions are worked on his own situation, especially in the context of illness. Far from being an impediment, his fever and fatigue are frequently a trigger, paradoxically providing a necessary flux of strength or an ease of detachment from himself: 'Une fois mes membres fatigués installés, moi je déserte. Et au travail' (*FF*, p. 215). Condemned to total immobility in bed and feeling the ravages of boredom tilting the balance of his personality, he plays his game of poetic power politics: operating on his cranium and flattening it over a wide area, he brings out his mental cavalry, watches their movements and listens to their hooves until, enthused by their rhythmic ardour, he is restored to equilibrium. The pain caused by a whitlow is aggravated by the fact that he is in a hotel and cannot cry out during the night: so, out of his skull, he wheels the bass drums, the brass section and a resonant organ-like instrument which set up the most deafening orchestral perform-ance, within which he can safely bury his cries. Or it may be in his dealings with others that, with the same rhythmic gusto and pulsations of will, he exteriorizes the pressure of an unresolved situation:

Je peux rarement voir quelqu'un sans le battre. D'autres préfèrent le monologue intérieur. Moi, non. J'aime mieux battre.

Il y a des gens qui s'assoient en face de moi au restaurant et ne disent
rien, ils restent un certain temps, car ils ont décidé de manger.
En voici un.
Je te l'agrippe, toc.
Je te le ragrippe, toc.
Je le pends au porte-manteau.
Je le décroche.
Je le repends.
Je le redécroche.
Je le mets sur la table, je le tasse et l'étouffe. (*LNR*, p. 104)

A second area of Michaux's magic might be termed transub-
stantiation, wilful or spontaneous. Few poets have shown his
inclination to eliminate himself for a purpose, to make the
transition into other forms and substances and, in so doing, to
penetrate the secret textures of inanimate life and the animal
world: 'Il fait, de façon unique, abandon de son être d' ''homme'''
(*L'Herne*, p. 339). Another text entitled 'Magie' recounts how he
relieved his nervous disposition and found tranquillity by entering
an apple. For years he made no progress, baulked perhaps by
some false notion of self-respect, but then tried a less direct
approach, conquering his tendency towards distraction and
fragmentation by first uniting himself with the river Scheldt at
Antwerp and then switching to the apple, an achievement
marked by an intense focus of suffering culminating in personal
anaesthesia: 'Quand j'arrivai dans la pomme, j'étais glacé' (*Pl*,
p. 10). More frequently, he adopts animal forms. 'Les animaux
et moi avions affaire ensemble', he writes, 'Mes mouvements je
les échangeais en esprit, contre les leurs, avec lesquels, libéré de la
limitation du bipède, je me répandais au-dehors...' (*Pass*, p. 200).
He describes, in 'L'Etranger parle', how such transmigration
may be used, not necessarily to give greater expansiveness or
freedom of movement, but to provide a more economical physical
form (that of the 'puce préventive', for example) in moments of
weakness or drained energy, thus enabling one to recuperate:
'Merveilleuse réduction. Le Monde animal trouve ainsi une
nouvelle séduction auprès de ceux-là mêmes qui l'avaient tenu en
mépris' (*FV*, p. 110).
    Closely allied, though working essentially through self-
withdrawal instead of self-projection, are Michaux's various
techniques of immunization. It may be a case of clenching himself

into a ball or circle to such a degree of density and self-sufficiency
that he cannot even see external reality two yards away. Of such
moments he says, in words reminding one of the function of his
buffer-states: 'Il me semble qu'un obus ou la foudre même
n'arriverait pas à m'atteindre tant j'ai de matelas de toutes parts
appliqués sur moi' (*Pl*, p. 11). Elsewhere, one finds the striking
phrase (implying a perfectly polished and perhaps circular
psychic surface which allows no hand-hold and repels all
boarders): 'Le poli psychique les préserve' (*FV*, p. 114). Alternatively, it may be a question of adjusting an inner tempo, as in
the case of 'La Ralentie' (*Pl*, p. 41) who finds it possible to
transcend fatigue, human contacts and the need for defensive
retreat through this secret of 'slowed-down' life. In the veiled
self-portrait, 'Portrait d'homme' (*L'Herne*, p. 338), Michaux
writes: 'Personne plus que lui n'a le sens de l'immobilité. La
matière la plus immobile, et qui pourtant vit et s'achève, l'arbre,
le fruit, sont ses amis'. At other times, possibly inspired by the
model of Chinese Taoism, it is more an act of self-effacement than
of self-withdrawal or self-immobilization, but the result is the
same: 'Un homme ainsi effacé n'est plus heurté ni par substances
ni par phénomènes' (*BA*, p. 187).

One final aspect of Michaux's poetic art is his inventive
detachment from himself, or what one might call 'experimental
schizophrenia'. He objectivizes his obsessions while experiencing
them, freezes into distracting patterns the very monstrosities of
the imagination which perturb him and reflect his deepest
instincts. He shows an uncanny ability to be simultaneously
committed and aloof, his own victim and his own observer. A
wish expressed in 'Portrait d'homme', absorbing the image of the
magic student in *Au Pays de la Magie* who can walk on both sides
of a river bank at the same time, is: 'Si on pouvait marcher à côté
de soi' (*L'Herne*, p. 339). In *Passages* (p. 45), speaking of a visual
dialogue with oneself, he tells how 'Ce radotage, infiniment
répété, de soi mis devant soi, plaît. Prolongé il constitue une cure'.
It is above the gap of this dialogue that Michaux performs the
precarious balancing-act of his poetry, achieving a *disponibilité*
with regard to himself which is virtually a form of salvation.

Whether he resorts to slowed-down rhythms or, taking
advantage of the fact that 'La vitesse remplace le poids et fait fi
du poids' (*Pl*, p. 130), turns the mind into a weightless projectile;

whether he works by anaesthesia or inflammation; whether he withdraws from the world behind an impenetrable mattress of psychic energy or galvanizes himself by means of frenzied intervention; whether he employs the techniques of the yogi or those of the black magician, Michaux's 'magic' is almost invariably a response to a problem of equilibrium. It is thanks to its infinite resources that, if not a perfect, then a liveable balance of power can be maintained, holding the pressures of internal and external reality in a state of reasonably peaceful coexistence and allowing him to say in 'Fin d'un domaine': 'Pour une raison ou une autre, il n'y a jamais d'exode massif des miens, ni non plus d'entrée massive de population ennemie' (*FV*, p. 214). Similarly he writes: 'Sans les travaux de drainage et d'irrigation alternés et savamment équilibrés, le domaine souffre' (*FV*, p. 215). Michaux has made poetry the most adjustable instrument of drainage and irrigation, controlling the inlet and outlet valves along the frontiers of his property and governing the exchanges between his own domain and hostile territory.

Yet one may wonder how permanently satisfying, for the man who has said 'Mais le chiqué ne peut valoir le naturel' (*BA*, p. 124), poetic magic and its illusionist's tricks can be;[22] and in a 1958 essay Michaux sums up his potentialities for real achievement in noticeably modest, not to say belittling, terms: 'Mais en magie...qui n'est pas fort est victime. Pour une offensive, j'aurais vingt fois à être sur la défensive, et quatre-vingt-dix-neuf fois serais distrait' (*Pass*, p. 217).

SPIRITUALITY AND DUALITY

Throughout the poet's work there runs the desire for an experience more absolute than the provisional *ad hoc* measures of his poetic magic. His ideal, one could say, is a deeper, more authentic form of mental hygiene. The traveller in the Pays de la Magie circulates on the fringe of occult messages which hold a key to something more essential than his present relationship with the inhabitants; the 'Capitale Fédérale' (*Aill*, p. 192), with its promise of arrival at the centre of power, remains fog-bound and inaccessible; and when, on the 'Jours de la Grande Purification' (*Aill*, p. 233-4), rivers of flame move through the streets of the capital, even those of high repute in certain brands of magic are devoured by the stream of nothingness, which brings an abrupt end to the 'foisonnement des formes brunes de la magie'. Michaux tells how the Indian mystic Milarepa began himself by black magic: 'Il commença par là, c'est la règle. Ensuite, il expia' (*BA*, p. 92)—so suggesting a more worthy spiritual state beyond the acquisitive clutches of mental magic and to which they are a mere antechamber. In a recent essay the author has debated the relative merits and possible compatibility of *jeu* and *méditation*. On the one hand the spirit of play, releasing one from the arbitrary combinations of reality, is an invaluable means of 'liberté d'action', a genie of possibility. On the other hand he sees the inadequacy of his waking dreams as stemming from the very excess of play, personal intervention, movement and variation: 'Ce trop qu'il faudrait enlever à mes rêves vigiles, c'est le *jeu*. Pour méditer, il faut se retenir de jouer. Alors tout change' (*FF*, p. 223). And he goes on to describe the contemplation of the gourou which, instead of moving between a multiplicity of images, attaches itself to a single image such as the expanding lotus flower in order to be drawn into 'le sans image' and, ultimately, into the miracle of 'VIDE-SUBSTANCE', the perfect reconciliation of presence and absence, fullness and void, sustenance and annihilation.

In its early development, Michaux's spiritual sensitivity contains a strong Christian strain. His autobiographical glimpses show the importance of the notion of saintliness and the prestige of such figures as the 'curé d'Ars', Saint Joseph of Cupertino and Ruysbrœk. The history of his *alter ego* A. leans on the explanation of paradise lost and a fall from grace; and 'l'Insoumis' wonders 'comment il pourrait rentrer dans le paradis perdu (et qu'importe que ce soit parfois un enfer)' (*Pl*, p. 68). In Ecuador opium is rejected in favour of ether, with its violent separation of parts: 'plus chrétien; arrache l'homme de soi' (*Ec*, p. 106). In India, while admiring the serene, self-possessed *extase* of Hindu religion, he never ceases to feel the attraction of Christian mysticism, with its tortured duality and self-abolition by humiliation:

Sainte Angèle de Foligno, saint François d'Assise, sainte Lydwine de Schiedam arrivaient par déchirement, *Ruysbrœk l'Admirable, saint Joseph de Cupertino,* par une humilité effrayante, et, à force d'être rien et dépouillés, étaient happés par la Divinité... (*BA*, pp. 27–8) an attraction borne out by a poem such as 'Clown' (*ED*, 249–50) where, after a process of self-inflicted indignities, the protagonist imagines himself plunged into 'l'infini-esprit',

> à force d'être nul
> et ras...
> et risible...

Allusions to Christ are not uncommon, sometimes as simple *points de repère*, sometimes more significantly linked, if only in an ironical or belittling way, to the image of his own martyrdom:

> Je me suis bâti sur une colonne absente.
> Qu'est-ce que le Christ aurait dit s'il avait été fait ainsi?
>
> (*Ec*, p. 99)

A. sees his fate in terms of the cross; one of the 'Meidosems' stands crucified; the woman in the clearing, threatened by a massive bird of prey, is 'arquée sur une croix' (*VP*, p. 226); and above all (though Michaux has said[23] that he composed the work when the question of Christ did not interest him overmuch) there is the exodus of multiple crucified figures of *Quatre cents hommes en croix* (1956). In more recent years and especially since his explorations with hallucinogenic drugs, Michaux has tended to explain his work with increasing reference to Oriental religions, especially Hinduism. But there is no doubt that this spiritual sensitivity transcends any specific religious form, Christian, Hindu or other. The poet has stated categorically enough: 'Foi, semelle inusable pour qui n'avance pas' (*LNR*, p. 84). And in *Un Barbare en Asie*, in the heart of his enthusiasm for new cultures with secrets in the art of *la vie intérieure*, he stays fully conscious of the limitations of religion. The faithful in India are the same as the faithful anywhere, people whose spiritual impetus is lost in convention and collective mediocrity, 'qui, comme la plupart des gens occupés de religion, arrivés à un certain niveau, pataugent et jamais ne vont au-delà' (*BA*, p. 27). The southern Hindus 'ont une préférence pour les dieux à petite divinité' (*BA*, p. 116), a lament to be sung for almost every other race on earth. The Temple of the Five Hundred Buddhas in Canton earns the bathetic comment: 'Cinq cents! s'il y en avait seulement un de bon! un vrai de vrai' (*BA*, p. 151). Just as he is looking for something beyond magic, so he is looking for something more than gods.

Michaux's spirituality is synonymous with an obsession with Infinity. Perhaps it derives initially from that same sense of lack which leaves a bottomless hole in his life:

> A cause de ce manque, j'aspire à tant.
> A tant de choses, à presque l'infini...
> *(LNR*, p. 92)

It is an obsession which takes on innumerable poetic expressions. At the most elementary level, it is the urge to be redeemed from the limits and superfluity of his own nature:

> Présence de soi: outil fou
> On pèse sur soi
> On pèse sur sa solitude
> ...
> On pèse sur le vide.
> *(Pl*, p. 99)

In an essay on ether, he speaks of man's underestimated need to be conquered, to rid himself of his own reserves of strength as if asphyxiated by them. Some, he says, are more insatiable than others and look far beyond the ideal of human love as a satisfactory 'absolution': 'Il arrive cependant à l'un ou l'autre de vouloir perdre davantage son Je, d'aspirer à se dépouiller, à grelotter dans le vide (ou le tout). En vérité, l'homme s'embarque sur beaucoup de bateaux, mais c'est là qu'il veut aller' *(LNR*, p. 65). This act of 'self-stripping', divesting the self of will-power, personal preferences, mental screens and all that might stand as a protective intermediary between the individual and the universal, has a model in Hindu prayer: 'Tout vêtement retranche du monde. Tandis qu'étendu, nu dans l'obscurité, le *Tout* afflue à vous, et vous entraîne dans son vent' *(BA*, p. 44). But as in Mallarmé's poetry, which reaches constantly towards the fringe of 'le Rien qui est la vérité',[24] one never knows whether this absolute is Being or Nothingness, 'le vide (ou le tout)'. Most often Michaux sees it as void, Nirvana. In the grip of ether one is thrown 'dans l'immense bouche du vide, au-delà de toute possible critique, où l'on se perd, ami ou ennemi, vide, grand autrui à qui on peut se rendre sans lâcheté, sans honte' *(LNR*, p. 70). The tormented energy of the apocalyptic poem 'L'Avenir' *(LNR*, pp. 199–200) finally fades out in the ideal of a dissolution of all compartments and total abolition within immeasurable space:

> Plus jamais.
> Oh! vide!
> Oh! Espace! Espace non stratifié... Oh! Espace, Espace!

The poem 'Mon Dieu' (*LNR*, p. 198) ends similarly with the prospect of an ultimate purification and the annihilation of the self as a separate identity. It has the same tone of yearning invocation:

> Oh! poids! Oh! anéantissement!
> Oh! pelures d'Etres!
> Face impeccablement ravissante de la destruction!
> Savon parfait, Dieu que nous appelons à grands cris.
> Il t'attend ce monde insolemment rond. Il t'attend.
> Oh! aplatissement!
> Oh! Dieu parfait.

Like Rimbaud who, in the crisis of *Une Saison en Enfer*, says 'Ah! je suis tellement délaissé que j'offre à n'importe quelle divine image des élans vers la perfection',[25] Michaux willingly abandons his non-fulfilment to any available infinite force: 'Grand, j'aimerais aller vers plus grand encore, vers l'absolument grand. Je m'offre s'il existe. J'offre mon néant suspendu, ma soif jamais encore étanchée, ma soif jamais encore satisfaite' (*FV*, pp. 221–2). In certain poems the force of salvation is seen as a supreme second person. 'Mais Toi, quand viendras-tu?' (*Pl*, pp. 97–8) calls on a perhaps non-existent sovereign power to burst open his hollow world, twist his aimless horizontality into the vertical plane, project him dynamically upwards and explode him finally into the anonymity of infinite space:

> Tu viendras, si tu existes,
> appâté par mon gâchis,
> mon odieuse autonomie;
> Sortant de l'Ether, de n'importe où, de dessous mon moi bouleversé, peut-être;
> jetant mon allumette dans Ta démesure,
> et adieu, Michaux.

In 'Comme pierre dans le puits' (*Pl*, pp. 99–100) the coveted experience is conceived of in liquid rather than spatial terms.

Whether it is primarily self-affirmation or self-abolition remains ambiguous, but the aim, to find relief from tension in a quasi-divine body greater than his own, is the same:

> Je cherche un être à envahir
> Montagne de fluide, paquet divin,
> Où es-tu mon autre pôle? Etrennes toujours remises,
> Où es-tu marée montante?
> Refouler en toi le bain brisant de mon intolérable tension!
> Te pirater.

The desire for a personal 'other pole' recurs in the poet's writing. He speaks of that 'besoin de l' "Autre", l'introuvable Autre' (*LNR*, pp. 68–9) which forms an aching hollow in the human personality and describes himself as

> Cherchant je ne sais quoi de personnel,
> Je ne sais quoi à m'adjoindre dans cette infinie matière invisible et compacte. (*LNR*, pp. 184–5)

Indeed, although it is said in 'Portrait d'homme' (*L'Herne*, p. 338) that 'Il est pressé de se défaire du peu de forces qui lui reste. Il est ivre de néant—pas d'amour', Michaux's ideal is frequently evoked in terms of love and unity with a transcendent feminine presence. His earlier work is alive with poetic references to a mysterious ethereal partner. 'L'impossible retour' (*FV*, pp. 236–9) reads:

> …et toujours on me retenait, on ne me permettait pas de rentrer dans ma patrie. J'avais mal, j'avais mal à ma poitrine, où une grande voile toujours tendue me poussait vers mon amie, la très secrète, la merveilleuse, celle qu'on ne peut nommer, celle dont on ne peut faire le tour, celle à qui on ne peut jamais assez se rafraîchir.

The concluding lines are a climax of subtlety and grace, creating a female figure as enchanting and provocative as any in Surrealist poetry, by Breton or Aragon, Eluard or Desnos:

> On me retenait, on me tenait dans la souffrance, loin de la patrie où la fille des cascades m'attendait, fine comme le jonc, forte comme un chêne, compliquée comme la Chine, semblable à une lame, rayon qui traverse les barques, ange des clairs abîmes.

In 'L'Etranger parle', as if allowing his imagination to explore at length what only crossed his page sixteen years before as a cryptic

reference to 'l'après-midi de "la fiancée se retire" ' (*Pl*, p. 16),
Michaux portrays ardent lovers who, 'punis d'avoir mal aimé',
are repelled from each other by some supernatural allergy or,
instead of relieving each other's pains, can only transfer them:
'Angoissée, déchirée, la fiancée à son tour oubliant tout amour,
ne veut plus que fuir, échapper à ces bras si terriblement, si
incompréhensiblement meurtriers' (*FV*, p. 103).

A remarkable feature of Michaux's evocations of the beyond
is the multiplicity of imagery provoked, both within individual
poems and from poem to poem. In 'Mais Toi, quand viendras-
tu?' the divine force is apprehended variously as thunder, a
clawing hand, a boring-machine, an erector of cathedrals, a
projector of shells, something descending, something ascending,
an explosive gas, a hand which throws the match from the outside
into that explosive gas, a supernatural windfall, something expanding outwards beyond bounds, something 'homing in' in con-
densed form. In 'Comme pierre dans le puits', the all-containing
being is a liquid mountain, a magnetic pole, a wrapped gift and
a rising tide, and the poet's rôle is simultaneously one of conquest
and defeat, self-possession and self-loss. The magical 'fille des
cascades' is slenderness and strength, simplicity and complexity,
line and intertwine, the liquid and the luminous, the vegetal and
the metallic, light and dark, the natural and the supernatural.
Infinity itself may be experienced as transparent crystalline space,
ethereal yet endowed with mineral hardness, an 'Espace-cristal'
(*FV*, p. 221). Or it may be liquid, an expression of that mysterious
'mer sans eau, mais non pas sans vagues, mais non pas sans
étendue' (*LNR*, p. 94) which underlies so many of the poet's
departures: 'Alors dans un océan de bonheur, nous nous unissons
à *Lui*. Qui, *Lui*?' (*FV*, p. 116). Or spatial and liquid qualities
may be brought together in images of fog, fine mist or the
nebulous breath. In *Ecuador* (pp. 90–1) Michaux, speaking of
ether and its 'lait de brume', tells how it stitches together the
tears in his personality and unifies him: 'Ah ce n'était que ça,
l'Infini! Ah! Cependant le brouillard me reprise...Infini, infini
quand même'; while in 'La jeune fille de Budapest' (*Pl*, p. 85)
the poet accedes to weightlessness and fluidity of movement by
entering a woman's breath: 'Dans la brume tiède d'une haleine
de jeune fille, j'ai pris place'. In 'Clown' (*ED*, p. 250), he feels
opened to absorb 'une nouvelle et incroyable rosée'; while in one

of the 'Tranches de savoir' he celebrates a similar supernatural sustenance, to be drunk from the air:

> Pour boire dans le corps d'un infusoire, il faut se faire petit, petit-petit, comme d'ailleurs pour toute découverte importante. Mais quelle nourriture alors, légère, fine, aérienne, substance de substance, et dont, qui l'a goûté, jamais plus ne se peut désenivrer. (*FV*, p. 55)

Sometimes the experience is utter silence. At other times it is sound, the strains of a deep unalterable harmony which seep into his corporal frame and claim it as their own: 'Dans le fond de nos os, on fait chanter le Chant profond. C'était si simple. On l'attendait depuis si longtemps. Je ne peux pas vous expliquer...' (*FV*, p. 117). Sometimes it is described as sheer emptiness. At other times it is like a vast tangible fabric: 'On ne travaille plus. Le tricot est là, tout fait, partout' (*Pl*, p. 43). And in a startling image which combines suggestions of the whiteness of fog, purity and oceanic folds, as well as providing an analogy to Michaux's matchstick, a diminutive foreign body thrown into volatile space, he sees himself as an insect or bed-bug caught in the sheets: 'Fais signe si tu existes, viens, me prenant comme insecte dans une couverture, viens tout de suite' (*FV*, p. 222). Sometimes it is an 'aplatissement': the clown of the poem of that title undergoes 'un nivellement parfait' and is 'Anéanti quant à la hauteur' (*ED*, pp. 249–50). At other times it is infinite upthrust: he is projected 'comme obus dans la voie verticale' (*Pl*, p. 97); an insurmountable cathedral rears up from his own unsubstantiality; and he finds himself on 'le grand escalier sans fin' (*FV*, p. 230) or climbing the hundreds of storeys of a royal palace disappearing in absolute silence into the clouds (*LNR*, p. 26). Sometimes the predominant emphasis is on the abolition of boundaries. At other times the poet is taken into the perfect ball or circle, able to hear 'le chant de la sphère'. The culminating words of 'Agir, je viens' (*FV*, pp. 32–5), reconciling the ideas of infinite expanse and containment, unlimited movement and a rounded self-sufficiency, are:

> Où étaient les verrous est l'océan ouvert
> L'océan porteur et la plénitude de toi
> Intact, comme un œuf d'ivoire;

and 'Entre centre et absence' (*Pl*, pp. 36–7) ends with a beautiful image fusing the various motifs of air and water, space and roundness, invisibility and contour: 'C'était à l'arrivée, entre centre et absence, à l'Euréka, dans le nid de bulles...'.

Two superb texts illustrate at its richest the drama of spiritual aspiration and frustration in Michaux: *Portrait des Meidosems* (first published as *Meidosems* in 1948) and *L'Espace aux ombres* (first published in 1952). The Meidosems are a fascinating imaginary race similar in some respects to those which have appeared in the author's *Ailleurs*. But all the surrounding social structures and 'real-life' physical trappings which go to create the illusion of a real journey in a real country have disappeared, and the work does not adopt the convention of the travelogue. In fact, the Meidosems have no fixed physical form. They move pliably from one shape to another: thirty-four tangled lances, bubbles, lianas, a sponge, a mist on a mirror, hundreds of electrified wires, projectiles, a cluster of sparks. And their domain is no more precise than the elements, earth, air, fire and water, with which they interpenetrate spasmodically and inconclusively. Indeed, they are no more than living metamorphosis and their life is played out 'entre centre et absence', between shape and shapelessness, definition and lack of definition, the urge for an ultimate state of being and a host of provisional postures. They are an intermediary people, if they can be called a people at all, doomed to a constant shuttle-service between their own substance and dreams of unsubstantiality: 'D'une brume à une chair, infinis les passages en pays meidosem...' (*VP*, p. 171). They alternate between the terrible affliction of 'Roche d'âme' (*VP*, p. 180), movements as laborious as those of gigantic pachyderms, or moments when a great diagonal lance fixes them to the ground; and the ecstasy of rising up through trees in the form of sap, the joy of germination when they float in the air like thistledown, or moments when they transmute themselves into waterfalls or fire. The Meidosem aspires to be elsewhere and other, but cannot deny the backward glance and the call of his own nature, deceptively left behind: 'âme à regrets et projets, âme pour tout dire' (*VP*, p. 134). He shoots away like a shell, faster than the eye can see, but he has not really left: 'Oh non, il n'est même pas parti. Il n'est parti que de sa marche d'âme' (*VP*, p. 136). The tyrannical force of the solid, which holds him there in frustrated broken bottle-ends of himself, is his most fundamental need; and the implanted lance, which seems to be there to kill him, may be his only support. But from this ambiguous knot of torture and elasticity, imprisonment and evasion, immobility and *élan*, despair and unquenchable aspiration, there rises a final hymn of possibility:

> Des ailes sans têtes, sans oiseaux, des ailes pures de tout corps volent vers un ciel solaire, pas encore resplendissant, mais qui lutte fort pour le resplendissement, trouant son chemin dans l'empyrée comme un obus de future félicité.
>
> Silence. Envols.
>
> Ce que les Meidosems ont tant désiré, enfin ils y sont arrivés. Les voilà. (*VP*, p. 206)

L'Espace aux ombres moves even further away from the recognizable physical world. Its setting is a strange intermediary zone in mental or metaphysical space, possibly a kind of purgatory. Its protagonists are souls or spirits who have passed beyond the confines of life but have not yet found a reliable relationship with the forces which move through and beyond this 'space between'. Like the Meidosems, these are souls 'entre centre et absence', and the work is similarly an imaginative experience of tormented duality. 'Ne m'en demandez pas trop', pleads the narrative voice, 'quoique loin de terre, je suis plus loin encore du centre' (*FV*, p. 181). It is a frightening 'other world'. Souls flounder impotently as they are tracked down by 'les *Rapaces de l'Invisible*' (*FV*, p. 170) or spiritually gutted by 'des âmes excavatrices, traversant l'espace' (*FV*, p. 175); others are carried by the wrong current to be congealed in the zone of thick jelly, or swept into the spiritual doldrums of 'la mer des lassitudes' (*FV*, p. 173); there are decapitated souls, wounded souls who will be forever gaping, souls who have tried too hard to preserve their own unity and are now nothing but an enormous sound doomed to roll around for centuries before disappearing into absolute silence. The narrator herself is forced to fall silent as the very act of speech or even thought becomes infinitely dangerous. It is not lightly that she says: 'L'espace, mais vous ne pouvez concevoir cet horrible en dedans-en dehors qu'est le vrai espace' (*FV*, p. 190). One belongs to a place, uncircumscribed and undefined, where one is simultaneously within and without, self and not-self, fullness and total hollowness, self-possessed and dispossessed. One can conceive of oneself as a separate entity while everything proves that one is not. And yet this space has an attraction beyond the ordinary. The narrator tentatively explains her continuing torment in this way:

> Je me mets en travers peut-être des courants de l'Infini. Je dois sûrement me mettre en travers, c'est la raison de ma nuit.
>
> D'autres âmes, ne se questionnant pas, 'se présentant' bien à l'afflux, en un instant sont emportées par la grande, l'invisible avalanche qui sans cesse roule vers le centre entraînant celles qui sont prêtes. (*FV*, p. 173)

Nor does she doubt that 'les eaux courantes de fleuves inconnus vous penchent, vous emportent au loin, si vous savez les utiliser' (*FV*, p. 185). Signs are always at hand that this is the vast and turbulent antechamber to the Essential. One brushes momentarily against 'la bénéfique', a feminine presence with her accompanying 'abîme de joie' (*FV*, p. 179); one's thoughts turn, although there is no proof that it exists, to 'L'ondée tant attendue, l'ondée d'infini, qui apaisera l'âme' (*FV*, p. 187); and the intuition is firmly rooted that the harmonies of a superior form of knowledge pervade these parts: 'Savoir, autre savoir ici, pas *Savoir* pour renseignements. *Savoir* pour devenir musicienne de la Vérité' (*FV*, p. 189). Despite her awesome martyrdom, the speaking spirit would not exchange it for less:

> Non, non l'infini et l'avant-coureur d'infini est un tel soulagement ici que, pour rien au monde, je vous le jure, pour rien au monde je ne voudrais regagner le vôtre, qu'on n'a pas oublié, allez, débité en tranches, en tranches inégales et surprenantes, monde de la distraction, racine jamais abreuvée. (*FV*, p. 177)

No French poet since Baudelaire has studied human duality with such refinement. 'C'est moi le bon poignard qui fait deux partout où il passe' (*LNR*, p. 181), Michaux writes. Images of man's 'sort à deux têtes' (*FV*, p. 218) or what one of his titles calls 'la vie double' (*EE*, p. 119) are abundant in his work. The disinherited monsters known as the 'trunk-men', dwarf-beings unable to push out external limbs or antennae, are nevertheless dense containers of prayers and supplications: 'La fierté de leurs troncs dans la pauvreté de leurs moyens d'expression est sans pareille' (*EE*, p. 110); and though one cannot see what they are dependent upon, one is at a loss to imagine how they could possibly be independent. One of the poet's 'Dessins commentés'

(*LNR*, p. 45) shows a majestic head perfectly formed like an 'œuf d'ivoire', but 'Sur un tout autre plan quoique près de lui court à toute vitesse un clown aux jambes de laine': a striking juxtaposition of the contemplative and the active, the serene and the frenetic, the self-contained and the dispersed, the unified and the flailing, the sublime and the ridiculous. At other times duality is expressed as a drama of departure and return, upsurge and relapse: 'Que d'envols! Que de chutes!' (*VP*, p. 91). The narrator (*VP*, pp. 74–5) whose leg has stretched a hundred yards from his body in a vast hangar only to be retrieved urgently as shambling workmen enter dropping their tools, knows the frustration of an easy extension into space which turns into potential horror and must be reversed at all costs. Or it may be the dream of totality (the circle) which turns into a nightmare of contradiction (the cross): 'Il faut récupérer au loin le fils prodigue parti pour le cercle enchanté et qui revient lourdement portant la croix' (*LNR*, p. 69). The poet himself is a welding of two personalities, a grotesque two-headed hybrid, an inseparable *mélange* of spirit and matter, mental apprehension and corporal dissolution, self-possession and self-evacuation, containment and void:

Il en est bien embarrassé de sa double-tête et bien mieux s'en tirerait avec une seule.
Une pour penser, ça va. Une à l'autre bout pour évacuer, c'est moins bien. (*EE*, p. 111)

In a way reminiscent of Baudelaire's 'L'Héautontimorouménos', Michaux sees himself simultaneously as 'bourreau et victime de soi-même'. 'Je voudrais bien savoir pourquoi je suis toujours le cheval que je tiens par la bride' (*VP*, p. 235), he writes; and 'C'est moi qui suis le potier...je me creuse moi-même' (*VP*, p. 112); and 'Je m'aperçus bientôt que non seulement j'étais les fourmis mais aussi j'étais leur chemin' (*LNR*, p. 129). Much of his work is written at the crossroads of contradictory impulses, impulses such as those encapsulated in the brief text 'Dans les limbes lumineuses' (*VP*, pp. 83–4), where the poet is again 'translated' into a feminine spirit:

Liberée
enchaînée

accablée, accédant à l'accalmie
ou furieuse, frappant du maillet le front de l'opposant.
Etalée
ramassée
épanchée
s'anastomosant.

But the last word, providing an appropriate note of perseverance, belongs to the following quotation: 'Ces entrecroisements étaient notre inquiétude, notre tristesse, notre joie, notre enrichissement, notre perte, notre étonnement, notre confusion. Nos espoirs aussi' (*VP*, p. 99).

In delving deeper and deeper into the expressions of his own duality, Michaux has at the same time revitalized Classical myth and its images of the human condition: the myths of Sisyphus, Tantalus, Prometheus, the vessels of the Danaides, the labyrinth and so on. 'Chacun ses travaux forcés' (*EE*, p. 105), he says. There is the glutinous one-legged monster doomed to climb a pole extending into the infinite, hating the pole and staying as far away from it as possible but hating space even more and therefore desperate not to let go; or the hermaphrodite laboriously mounting a stairway which will lead nowhere. The poet is condemned to knock down wall after wall after wall without ever breaking from his prison; or, banished to 'le lieu du morne et de l'enroulé et de la reprise indéfinie', he watches a woman taking off a blouse to reveal another blouse which she take off to reveal another blouse, 'et le repos de la nudité n'arrive jamais' (*VP*, p. 214). The most ardent lovers repel each other magnetically; those most anxious to arrive are nailed to the ground within sight of the promised land which they will contemplate henceforth 'en tumultueux désirs' (*FV*, p. 104) but never attain. The poet is called on to tackle the new labours of Hercules: 'Et je dois nouer des papillons! C'est fatal, on me demande toujours ce que je ne sais pas faire' (*FV*, p. 234); 'Scaphandrier voulant saisir une épingle pleure ou tremble' (*FV*, p. 54); 'Ne pas se laisser condamner à défaire les chignons de bronze' (*FV*, p. 41); '"Poursuivez le nuage, attrapez-le, mais attrapez-le donc", toute la ville paria, mais je ne pus l'attraper' (*Pl*, p. 49). It is in images such as these that Michaux's poetry claims a mythical and universal dimension.

EXPERIMENTAL CONQUEST

'J'aurais pourtant voulu être un bon chef de laboratoire, et passer pour avoir bien géré mon "moi" ' (*Pl*, p. 212): in emphasizing Michaux's spirituality, one should not underrate his rôle as a 'poetic scientist'. With the possible exception of Valéry, no one has done more in this century to bridge the gulf between poetry and science—not by pursuing the two activities as complementary but separate studies but by forging a new literary genre which is unmistakably poetic and scientific at the same time. Nor has anyone gone further in demystifying, not only the Romantic view of spirituality and the beyond, but the very nature of poetry itself by means of experiment and critical self-conquest. As Rimbaud said, pointing to the limitations of the Romantics, 'la chanson est si peu souvent l'œuvre':[26] contemporary poetry can no longer content itself with vague lyricism, but only with total self-knowledge. And despite the fact that Michaux has always found himself torn between a plurality of possible selves, it is hard to imagine a more resourceful and self-possessed 'manager' of the 'space within'. In 1950 he wrote: 'depuis plus de dix ans, je fais surtout de l'occupation progressive' (*Pass*, p. 142). He has systematically explored and occupied more and more of his inner territory, casting light into every passage of the labyrinth. He has not hesitated to provoke his mental machinery, subjecting it to all possible stimuli and forcing it to reveal its latent potential:

Penser! Plutôt agir sur ma machine à être (et à penser) pour me trouver en situation de pouvoir penser nouvellement, d'avoir des possibilités de pensées vraiment neuves.

Dans ce sens, je voudrais avoir fait de la pensée expérimentale. (*Pass*, p. 151)

The poet's discovery of the drug mescalin in 1956, which has led to a prolonged period of explorations of the effects of hallucinogenic substances, has opened the door in his work to an incomparable wealth of 'pensée expérimentale'. Mescalin itself, an offshoot of peyotl, a 'sacred' drug used by certain Central American Indians, has a strong quasi-religious ancestry. Aldous Huxley, in *The Doors of Perception*,[27] writes of it:

...it had always seemed to me possible that through hypnosis, for example, or autohypnosis, by means of systematic meditation, or else by taking the appropriate drug, I might so change my ordinary mode of consciousness as to be able to know, from the inside, what the visionary, the medium, even the mystic were talking about.

From what I had read of the mescalin experience I was convinced in advance that the drug would admit me, at least for a few hours, into the kind of inner world described by Blake.

Michaux, for his part, says: 'Je m'étais pourtant préparé à admirer. J'étais venu confiant' (*MM*, p. 15). Whatever his precise expectations, however, there seems no doubt that the poet has released the drug's energies, not in a devotional spirit but as an avid scientific observer, a tendency which becomes more and more confirmed through the four major mescalin texts: *Misérable miracle* (1956), *L'Infini turbulent* (1957), *Connaissance par les gouffres* (1961) and *Les grandes épreuves de l'esprit* (1966). Just as in the early 1930s ether 'dont il veut observer le théâtre en soi' (*LNR*, p. 69) is put to the test, so he begins *Misérable miracle* by declaring: 'Ceci est une exploration. Par les mots, les signes, les dessins. La Mescaline est l'explorée' (*MM*, p. 13). In *Connaissance par les gouffres*, although not totally ruling out the euphoric attractions, he says that he has taken lysergic acid, psilocybine, mescalin and hashish 'non spécialement pour en jouir, surtout pour les surprendre, pour surprendre des mystères ailleurs cachés' (*CG*, p. 179); and his most emphatic statement is his famous epigraph to the same work:

> Les drogues nous ennuient avec leur paradis.
> Qu'elles nous donnent plutôt un peu de savoir.
> Nous ne sommes pas un siècle à paradis.
>
> (*CG*, p. 9)

It is clear, from the very persistence of Michaux's association with mescalin over some fifteen years, from the animated tone of the texts devoted to it, and from the sheer vividness and effervescence of his style, that the poet has not been disappointed in his desire to find himself 'en situation de pouvoir penser nouvellement'. Only on the rarest occasion in *Ecuador* did he feel his 'virginité de vue, d'observation refaite pour ainsi dire' (*Ec*, p. 27); and at the time of his first mescalin experiments he confesses: 'Je m'ennuie vite à présent en voyage. Tant de déjà vu, et un certain vieillissement jusque dans l'œil peut-être!' (*MM*, p. 96). Mescalin, on the contrary, provides an incredible new projector for his inner cinema. He speaks of the 'écran inouï de ma vision' (*MM*, p. 28); he becomes the centre of a kaleidoscope in which his look probes and proliferates. Mental images, losing their customary pallor and laxity of association, rear up in splendid isolation with dramatic vigour. It is not here that he needs to say, 'Si je pouvais donner du relief à une province...' (*Ec*, p. 43). For the poet who sees poetry as the place of *mouvements, passages* and *parcours*, the drug opens the mind to new speeds, rhythms and trajectories: 'Elle excelle en parcours. Sans repos, non contemplative' (*MM*, p. 68); 'les passages (apparemment) planétaires d'un univers accéléré sont une des merveilles de la Mescaline' (*MM*, p. 80). The ideal of *vitesse* which runs through his work is amply satisfied by this indefatigable 'traverseuse d'espaces'. Freed from his own compartments and brake-powers, he becomes living movement: 'Je suis à nouveau devenu un trajet, trajet dans le temps' (*MM*, p. 120). On what he calls 'the day of the great opening', in the climax of his third major mescalin experiment, this is his ecstatic description:

...et de nouveau j'étais navigation, navigation avant tout, brillant d'un feu pur et blanc, répondant à mille cascades, à fosses écumantes et à ravinements virevoltants, qui me pliaient et me plissaient au passage. Qui coule ne peut habiter. (*MM*, pp. 49–50)

With its 'jets en avant perpétuels pour libérer davantage et avec un élan renouvelé' (*MM*, p. 39) and its 'maximas indéfiniment dépassés' (*IT*, p. 41), the drug offers an unprecedented experience of *élan, devenir* and *dépassement* (words all featuring prominently in Michaux's definitions of his poetics). Everything sacrificed to its influence undergoes an extension into the infinite: the single becomes multiple; time and space, seething with life, become immeasurable; the tiniest object is prolonged into a beyond. Infinity, it is proved, is not some quasi-divine resting-place, a quietistic state at one with the boundless, nor a classified and reassuring mathematical abstraction, but restless movement eternally running away from the advancing clutches of the human mind:

Cependant la poussée d'Infini toujours continue, en vous, sur vous, à travers vous, en tous sens infinifiant...un infini toujours en charge, en expansion, en dépassement, infini de gouffre qui incessamment déjoue le projet et l'idée humaine de mettre, par la compréhension, fin, limites et fermeture.

Ainsi sait faire la mescaline (si toutefois vous ne lui êtes pas obtus et résistant) vous projetant loin du fini, qui partout se décout, se montre pour ce qu'il est: une oasis créée autour de votre corps et de son monde, à force de travail, de volonté, de santé, de volupté, une hernie de l'infini. (*IT*, pp. 18–19)

Simultaneously, mescalin pursues a process of 'essentialization'. Objects, liberated from their piecemeal context and from the barely imprinted world of appearances, acquire such density and autonomy that one wonders if they are not indeed a foretaste of the absolute. A vision of whiteness, beyond all individual examples and variations, becomes total unadulterated whiteness: 'Blanc absolu. Blanc par-dessus toute blancheur. Blanc de l'avènement du blanc. Blanc sans compromis, par exclusion, par totale éradication du non-blanc' (*MM*, p. 23). Later, it is the turn of black. Sartre's Roquentin, disorientated and sick in a world of gratuitousness and contingency, vainly interrogates the blackness of a tree-root to see if it is black, almost black or more than black, only to find that the word dissolves senselessly in the face of existence and that the notion of black, like that of the circle, does not exist. Mescalin proves otherwise. As if accepted to live the Platonic Idea, Michaux experiences a supreme black 'sans zones de moindre noirceur, véritable condensé de nuit, ou plutôt nuit psychique c'est-à-dire absolue' (*IT*, p. 40), after which the return to the excessive variety of colours and tones in his own room can only appear trivial and unjustifiable to the newly initiated 'ascète du noir' (*IT*, p. 42). The drug soars beyond comparisons into the realm of the superlative. It knows no half measures. All that it does it does prodigiously: 'On est envahi de superlatifs. On étouffe de superlatifs. On hurlerait de superlatifs. On est immense et rayonnant de superlatifs' (*IT*, p. 17). It is partly for this reason that he can say: 'ce que j'y ai vu, même risible, compte encore, m'est plus réel et inoubliable que tous les pays que j'ai parcourus' (*IT*, p. 157).

Yet his first major encounter with mescalin is branded indelibly as a '*misérable* miracle', showing again the ambivalence of Michaux's world and his inescapable rôle as 'le bon poignard qui fait deux partout où il passe' (*LNR*, p. 181). Much of what is offered is an endless pageant of cheap and meaningless spectacle: 'Du clinquant, son spectacle'. All that he needs to do on occasions is uncover his eyes to bring to an end 'la sotte féerie' (*MM*, p. 15). Vast Himalayan ranges rear up interminably before the inner eye, 'ineptes mais immenses' (*MM*, p. 22). Perhaps like the yogi seen in India who seemed to have 'plus de talent que de personnalité' (*BA*, p. 82), mescalin dispenses enormity without grandeur, samples of the absolute without significance, and leaves a feeling of idiotic discrepancy: 'Il manquait à cette grande exhibition d'être grave à proportion de son étendue apparente. Immense sans grandeur' (*MM*, p. 44). The drug cannot halt, alter or apply to any purpose its pretentious demonstrations. It is an empty 'maximomaniac'. Its superlatives are 'superlatifs qui ne veulent rien dire' (*CG*, p. 15), or superlatives in an endless self-abolishing chain, 'faute de mieux, faute de meilleurs, de plus vrais, de plus super-superlatifs' (*IT*, pp. 17–18). Its movements of *élan* and *dépassement* are, paradoxically, imprisoned within an inalterable pattern, totally abstract and schematic, divorced from all human substance and meaning. Its alternations and repetitions invite no decision and arrive at no conclusion: 'Vous n'êtes absolument pas plus avancé après cinquante aller et retour qu'après le premier. Rien n'a mûri' (*CG*, pp. 28–9). Its dynamic *parcours*, pursued without rhyme or reason, cannot be anything but indiscriminate. Indeed, its Infinity is only a blind mechanism of infinity: 'La métaphysique saisie par la mécanique' (*MM*, p. 128). The accumulation of mechanistic vocabulary employed by Michaux is unmistakable: he speaks of 'la machine à himalayer' (*MM*, p. 22), warning himself to withhold anything essential from its 'engrenage fou'; of its 'Répétition de métronome enragé' (*IT*, p. 16). All that is fed into this machine, however abject, however ridiculous, receives its 'grace' of infinitization. It is in this sense that Huxley sees 'Eternity in a flower, Infinity in four chair legs and the Absolute in the folds of a pair of flannel trousers!'[28] Whatever one's thought, one's visual image of the moment, one's current obsession, it will launch it on the road to the absolute. It has no objective truth of its own to propose, apart from that of a scientific process, and will lend itself accidentally to any vision. So, one may be a visual ascetic liberated from the distractions of phenomena to contemplate the essence of black, or a victim caught, by an inadvertent thought in that direction,

4—HM * *

within the equally dictatorial essence of the idea of prison:
'Essentielle, votre prison est devenue invulnérable. Vous ne
pouvez plus en sortir' (*MM*, p. 151). Alternatively, after a period
of practice, one can learn to exploit the drug as a trick or game
and feed in one's own material, as in this example of 'leaping
fingers':

Euréka! Cette fois j'ai trouvé, j'y suis arrivé! Encore un essai, et un autre,
et encore. Ça devient un jeu, quoiqu'il soit toujours fatigant de planter
une image-mère, mais quand j'y arrive, les images-filles rappliquent de
tous côtés avec une précipitation d'une bande de babouins à qui on a
jeté des cacahuètes. (*IT*, p. 140)

The bathetic final image makes it clear that this is a poor miracle
of creativity. As one reads elsewhere: 'Des trois que nous étions,
aucun n'avait donc pris cela avec révérence, mais plutôt comme
un tour de prestidigitateur' (*MM*, p. 45). In fact, one is tempted
to see the experience of mescalin as a kind of metaphysical
Ecuador. Just as Michaux's first dabblings with ether provoked the
reaction, 'Ah ce n'était que ça l'Infini! Ah!' (*Ec*, p. 90), and his
encounter with a volcano crater the disenchanted

> Ah! Ah!
> Cratère? ah!
> On s'attendait à un peu plus de sérieux...
> (*Ec*, p. 121)

so his first dealings with mescalin's Infinite teeter on the brink of
triviality and anti-climax. Just as the spectacle of the real world
was an absurd decor with which he had nothing in common, so
he can say of this new dynamic inner display, 'on regarde, en
étranger, ce spectacle raté et mécanique, en se demandant si on
n'est pas bien sot de vouloir interpréter ce film ridicule' (*MM*,
p. 30). Just as, in the Napo region of the Amazon, 'Le sol mou
s'en fout, ne dit ni oui, ni non' (*Ec*, p. 136), so the drug does its
violent ploughing in an inner space, a mental terrain, which is
equally indifferent: 'De grands socs de charrue labourent un
espace qui s'en fout' (*MM*, p. 22). And just as in the imaginative
land of Grande Garabagne the tribe of the Ourgouilles suffers
from a terrible self-devouring and self-evacuating diarrhoea,
'diarrhée avec autophagie' (*Aill*, p. 121), so the experimenter of
Connaissance par les gouffres (p. 110) comes to know the sterility and
horror of a similar affliction on the purely mental plane: the self-

digesting vicious circle of 'autopsychophagie'. It is hardly surprising that one of his early conclusions is that all, the perception of external and internal phenomena alike, is illusion: 'Au sortir de la Mescaline on sait mieux qu'aucun bouddhiste que tout n'est qu'apparence. Ce qui était avant, n'était qu'illusion de la santé. Ce qui a été pendant était illusion de la drogue' (*MM*, p. 80).

In its own way, mescalin is a totalitarian state. In opening the mind to the infinite, it breaks down will-power, mental defences, desirable censorships and selective mechanisms (including one's choice of words). It ridicules and humiliates the self by throwing it into an inhuman tempo not its own: 'un incessant broiement infligé à une vitesse surhumaine qui lessive toute résistance' (*IT*, p. 99). It reminds man in the most torturing way of the extent to which he is a 'mutilé psychique' (*CG*, p. 231), ill-equipped to cope with the pace and enormity of Infinity which is there at every hand as his authentic element, once he condescends to abandon his prudish false positions. He becomes an 'être déchiré, en dentelles, cherchant vainement la psychosuture' (*IT*, p. 57). Time and again Michaux stresses the drug's anti-human nature. As it twists his horizontal into a vertical, or converts him from a self-contained sphere into a single line shattered into a thousand pieces as it rears forwards, he resists. He pokes his stick into its rapidly accelerating wheel, not knowing which constitutes the capitulation, to stop or to go on. He tries to cheat the mechanism by throwing, not his essential personality, but only unimportant titbits into the arena of its megalomania:

> Tout ce que vous présenterez à la schizo mescalinienne sera broyé. Ne vous présentez donc pas vous-même. Et ne lui présentez aucune idée vitale, car c'est horrible ce qu'elle en fait.
>
> Présentez le peu important, des images, de petites idées courantes.
>
> Sinon vous serez totalement inhabitable, vous faisant horreur, votre maison dans le torrent, objet de dérision pour vous-même. (*MM*, p. 131)

For the poet who admired the dynamism of Hindu religious thought in which 'Une prière est un rapt' (*BA*, p. 26), this proves to be a supernatural 'rapt rapt' (*CG*, p. 116) inflicted on himself. His experience in 'Etapes' and 'Bonheur bête' (*LNR*, pp. 47–9) at the hands of malicious divinities who took away his hammer and tools, his broken bottles and eagle's claws, his properties and ballast, is repeated here at the hands of a new 'enlève-insubordination': 'il m'enlevait bien mes pointes, mon impression-nabilité, mes différences soudaines de tonus. Il m'enlevait mon originalité' (*CG*, p. 47). For the war-time poet of *Epreuves, exorcismes* who chanted his opposition to the totalitarian spirit emasculating occupied France with the words:

> Tu n'auras pas ma voix, grande voix
> Tu n'auras pas ma voix, grande voix
> (*EE*, p. 13)

this becomes the opportunity for an equally desperate act of resistance against dictatorship, however coaxing or euphoric, as in the case of psilocybine, its invitations may be:

Je disais à voix haute: 'Je ne veux pas avaler ce gros caramel', 'Je ne veux pas de ce qui vient à moi avec prédication', 'Je ne veux pas de ce qui vient presque gentiment, mais puissamment, me tourner et me retourner'. Car je n'oubliais pas de ne vouloir pas.

Sous une tout autre forme que celle que je connaissais, c'était toujours de la drogue, c'est-à-dire un poison offrant qui propose: 'Paradis. Paradis pour toi si tu acceptes'. Ce paradis, car chaque drogue a le sien, était paradis d'obéissance pour devenir idéalement normal, soumis à l'esprit de groupe. (*CG*, p. 41)

Mescalin is at the same time the enemy of his own poetry. A restricted creative mechanism, it knows no variations of the art of composition. As a dealer in the abstract and schematic, it ruthlessly eliminates the suggestive and sensual properties of the imagination:

La Mescaline diminue l'imagination. Elle châtre l'image, la désensualise. Elle fait des images cent pour cent pures. Elle fait du laboratoire...

Aussi est-elle l'ennemie de la poésie, de la méditation, et surtout du mystère. (*MM*, p. 64)

It is for reasons such as these that his overall judgment in the foreword to *Misérable miracle* is: 'La Mescaline et moi, nous étions souvent plus en lutte qu'ensemble. J'étais secoué, cassé, mais je ne marchais pas' (*MM*, p. 15). And if it is true, as he says (*CG*, p. 65), that some are gifted for union and others for self-preservation, then it is clear that Michaux himself prizes his margin of opposition and independence. He resists the temptation to coincide with himself in an act of self-giving. He is only a false

Narcissus: 'Dans ma vie j'essaie (voulant observer), d'approcher le plus possible de moi, mais sans coïncider, sans me laisser aller, sans me donner' (*MM*, p. 124).

Michaux is not a natural believer. Unlike the Mexican Indian who says: 'Il conduit là où est Dieu' (*CG*, p. 65), he is not convinced by the divine properties of the chemical extract of a sacred plant: 'Quoi de surnaturel là-dedans? On quittait si peu l'homme. On se sentait plutôt pris et prisonnier dans un atelier du cerveau' (*MM*, p. 16). The mescalin texts are largely a demythification of divinity. One never escapes the impression that Michaux is treading, not hallowed ground, but the floor of a scientific workshop. And as one approaches *Les grandes épreuves de l'esprit* (1966) one is made increasingly aware of the human mind as an infinity of technical micro-operations and of the rôle of drugs as an adaptable instrument of inquiry. Lao Tzu's words: 'Gouvernez l'empire comme vous cuiriez un petit poisson' apply here in a new way. There is no question of the grand supernatural windfall or devotion to a 'paradis artificiel', but only of meticulous and unrelenting inner laboratory-work on the smallest scale: 'Jamais, jamais je ne dirai assez le côté modeste, instrumental de l'esprit, son travail d'ouvrier' (*GE*, p.13).

'Qu'est-ce que le cerveau ne tue pas?' (*LNR*, p. 74), asked Michaux of his early experience of ether. It is not easy to estimate if and when mescalin suffered this fate. Even at the time of *L'Infini turbulent* (1957) he wonders: 'N'a-t-on pas perdu son temps à examiner la mescaline—et perdu un autre temps à se juger et dépister soi-même à l'aide de la mescaline?' (*IT*, p. 201); and a 1964 essay, summing up the drug's achievements, values only a small sector of its activities, that of the trance: 'Le reste est imagerie, distraction, morcellement, piétinement, ratissage, emportements, impatiences, dysharmonies, dérapages, renverse-ments, éparpillements, échantillonnages, successions infernales qui font en somme destruction' (*IT*, p. 211). Indeed the poet's supreme moment is not one of self-abandonment to the uncom-promising pull of successive superlatives, but one when, without conscious effort or deliberate cultivation of mental antibodies, he manages spontaneously to cut off the drug's effects and dis-connect himself: 'Emerveillé. Les seuls beaux moments de ma vie' (*IT*, p. 62). In answer to his own question in 1971, 'Pourquoi

avoir cessé de prendre de la Mescaline?' he mentions its un-
manageability and its intrinsic contradictions; and while
suggesting that it might be useful to take some once or twice
every few years to ascertain one's current position, he confesses
that he has given up even this idea and concludes: 'Mettons que
je ne suis pas très doué pour la dépendance' (*MM*, p. 195).
From the very first experiments he has been quick to disavow
any addiction or lasting allegiance, saying:

> Un mot encore. Aux amateurs de perspective unique, la tentation
> pourrait venir de juger dorénavant l'ensemble de mes écrits, comme
> l'œuvre d'un drogué. Je regrette. Je suis plutôt du type buveur d'eau.
> Jamais d'alcool. Pas d'excitants, et depuis des années pas de café, pas de
> tabac, pas de thé. De loin en loin du vin, et peu. Depuis toujours, et de
> tout ce qui se prend, peu. Prendre et s'abstenir. Surtout s'abstenir. La
> fatigue est ma drogue, si l'on veut savoir. (*MM*, p. 170)

One accepts that drugs are for him only one means among many,
a further temporary stage in his unfinished exploration of himself
and *la condition humaine*.

Yet one wonders if this is the final word. Perhaps like the soul
of *L'Espace aux ombres* who says: 'Je me mets en travers peut-être
des courants de l'Infini. Je dois sûrement me mettre en travers,
c'est la raison de ma nuit' (*FV*, p. 173), the Michaux of *Misérable
miracle* has not mastered the essential currents. As he says:
'C'était atroce, parce que je résistais' (*MM*, p. 127). There is
evidence that, from *L'Infini turbulent* onwards, he succeeds more
and more in using mescalin as an ally and 'presenting himself'
well to the waves of Infinity. It is all a question of relinquishing
his rôle as observer and giving himself more like a priest, in a
mood of faith and abandonment. It is then that, beyond the
superficial visual extravagances, he comes to know contemplative
transport, dilation beyond bounds, authentic liberation and the
total equality of gift and receipt. His most remarkable experience
of supernatural ecstasy has an astonishing prelude: his vision of
the thousands of gods. Levitational in the air, animated by some
almost imperceptible rhythm, stretching in innumerable ranks
beyond all frontiers, they accept his self-offering with no
disharmony:

> J'étais rempli d'eux. J'avais cessé d'être mal rempli. Tout était parfait. Il
> n'y avait plus ni à réfléchir, ni à soupeser, ni à critiquer. Il n'y avait plus

à comparer. Mon horizontale était maintenant une verticale. J'existais en hauteur. Je n'avais pas vécu en vain. (*IT*, p. 72)

But what is still described here in terms of a *lien* and as a visual relationship is to be followed by an even deeper experience: his total involvement in a swelling rhythm without images which extends him beyond all self-awareness and joins him with the perfect creative motions of the universal continuum. He himself is continued through time and space, admitted as part of the infallible fabric of the ever-renewed Cosmos: 'L'extase, c'est coopérer à la divine création du monde' (*IT*, p. 79). This is his fluent lyrical finale:

> Au-dessus des résolutions et des irrésolutions
> au-delà des aspects
> là où il n'y a ni deux, ni plusieurs
> mais litanie, litanie de la Vérité
> du *Ce* dont on ne peut donner le signe
> au-delà de l'antipathie, du non, du refus
> AU-DELA DE LA PREFERENCE
> dans l'enchantement de la pureté absolue
> là où l'impureté ne peut être ni conçue, ni sentie, ni avoir de sens
> j'entendais le poème admirable, le poème grandiose
> le poème interminable
> le poème aux vers idéalement beaux
> sans rimes, sans musique, sans mots
> qui sans cesse scande l'Univers.
>
> (*IT*, pp. 81–2)

There is no doubt that, since this initial realization that 'ma vaine vie voyageuse s'engageait enfin sur la route miraculeuse' (*IT*, p. 77), Michaux has progressively exploited what he calls the 'onde métaphysique' (*MM*, p. 183) with its 'ondulations religieuses' (*CG*, p. 27), and deepened his contact with the state of *extase*. So much so that one wonders if he has not touched upon the answer to the tormented in-between life of his Meidosems or his souls tossed in intermediate space. Early in *L'Infini turbulent* he says that once the 'second state' of mescalin is well established all feeling of foreignness disappears, 'remplacée par l'impression d'un *autre* monde, au lieu qu'avant d'être pris entièrement par la mescaline, on se trouve *entre* deux mondes' (*IT*, p. 47). *Connaissance par les gouffres* goes further:

L'extase et l'extase seule ouvre l'absolument sans mélange, l'absolument
non interrompue par la plus infime opposition ou impureté qui soit le
moindrement, même allusivement, autre...
   Cela, cela seulement est 'le grand jeu', et peu importe alors qu'une
onde ou non aide cet univers autonome, où un transport, comparable à
rien de ce qui est de ce monde, vous maintient soulevé, hors des lois
mentales, dans une mer de félicité. (*CG*, pp. 31–2)

An essay added to *Misérable miracle* (pp. 183–7) describes the
'Ineffable Vide' which, stripping one of material attachments,
ambitions, personal properties and all contradiction or diversity of
impression, takes one into a Void which is plenitude, a subtrac-
tion which is infinite multiplication, an abolition which is
excess, a beatific state which is both perfection and perpetual
recreation, arrival and *dépassement*. The state is not only one 'où
l'on voit la non-dualité triompher de la dualité dans une exaltation enthousiaste' (*MM*, p. 191) or in which 'l'esprit, recueillant
"soi" et "non-soi" pareillement, se trouve dans un monisme de
fait' (*GE*, p. 125), but one which fulfils the intuition suggested in
earlier mescalin works of <u>an almost inconceivable reconciliation</u>
of existence and <u>essence, being and becom</u>ing, of which one can
say: 'Mais cet "enfin" n'était pas du repos' (*IT*, p. 77). After
such knowledge, says Michaux, one feels the need to stay dis-
sociated more permanently from the dispensable matter of
physical life: 'Naturel, ou surnaturel, ou provoqué, l'état
extatique, par la suite donne des incitations au détachement, des
tentations de dépouillement, d'abandon' (*MM*, p. 187). The
same urge has welled up in *L'Infini turbulent* (p. 91): '<u>Assez des</u>
<u>bagatelles de l'art.</u> Il me faut changer, dès demain, <u>entrer dans</u>
<u>la voie de la libération, la voie sainte</u>'. In this realization, the poet
comes closer than at any other point in his work to following
Buddha's teaching, advertised at the end of *Un Barbare en Asie*,
that one should remain henceforth 'COLLES A LA CONTEMPLATION'.
   The hallucinogenic experiments prove, however, that <u>extase</u>
<u>has more than one expression</u>: 'L'infini...peut être abordé selon
trois modes, selon le mode pur, selon le mode diabolique, selon
le mode démentiel. Le bienheureux infini, le pervers et satanique
infini, l'horrible et traumatisant infini' (*IT*, p. 21). These different
modes are separated by the slenderest thread. The Infinite can
take hold of any tendency in human nature, idealistic, perverse or
maniacal, and, eliminating all else, make it a tyrant. It may be a

question of accidentally 'feeding in' a wrong impulse which rapidly devours the whole personality, or of abandoning the self to the wrong wave or vibration: 'Si le rythme est majestueux, l'infini sera divin. Si le rythme est précipité, l'infini sera persécution, angoisse, fragmentation, affolant' (*CG*, p. 27). It is for this reason that mystics and contemplatives have so often struggled with the demoniacal (which they have exteriorized and personified and called the Devil). *Extase* can be 'ou cosmique ou d'amour, ou érotique, ou diabolique' (*CG*, p. 31). It can veer from 'le prodigieusement beau' to 'le prodigieusement effrayant' (*CG*, p. 195). It can take its cue 'du pôle sinistre et du pôle des béatitudes' (*CG*, p. 215). Michaux's description of his own experience of the 'satanical infinite' is extremely vivid. In a kind of temptation of Saint Anthony he is submerged in a universal slough of lascivious shapes, erotic images, invitations to profanity, perversity and debauchery. He is dissolved, without resistance, in an ultimate of pollution in which all that sets itself up as good or ideal in man is mocked and reduced to nothing by the absolute *anti-pur*, a supernatural orgy of sensual degradation. It is a state of sin, not with regard to a God (for the words 'Dieu' and 'Diable' Michaux substitutes 'l'opération divine' and 'l'opération démoniaque') but with regard to oneself, to the idea one would like to preserve of one's own dignity and divine potential. It is the revenge of the *moi pervers* inflicted on the *moi correct*. It is, in its own way, a supreme act of conscience, but a perverse act performed by 'une conscience du reste qui comme l'autre conscience *se scandalise*, mais du bien, de l'effort, de l'idéal, visage que les contemplatifs purs ont dû voir d'autant plus outré et mauvais, proportionné à la sainteté de leur premier "moi"' (*IT*, p. 178). Michaux, then, has not escaped from human duality through mescalin, but plumbed it in new depth and with a new comprehension. He has delved further than ever, further perhaps than any contemporary poet, into the mysteries which led Baudelaire to write: 'Il y a dans tout homme, à toute heure, deux postulations simultanées, l'une vers Dieu, l'autre vers Satan'.[29] His moments of transcendence have only refined this awareness. And in a manner quite different from *Meidosems* or *L'Espace aux ombres*, though equally colourful and fascinating, the drug texts are a complex study of the same fundamental issue: 'De l'insondable mal. De l'insondable dualité' (*IT*, p. 183).

Michaux's latest works have explored duality in yet another sense. For, while pushing further and further into transcendent states of being and all that stretches beyond the laborious clutches of the *premier moi*, they have also rediscovered the wonders of the normal self. A lyrical passage from *Misérable miracle*, describing the fading effects of mescalin, needs to be quoted at length:

> Je me retrouve petit à petit, sans m'être encore complètement récupéré, je m'éloigne de cette drogue, qui ne me convient pas. C'est moi, ma drogue, que celle-ci m'enlève.
>
> Je m'éloigne du changement de caractère qu'elle avait introduit en moi. Je reviens à ma lenteur, à mes filtres, aux ponts que je bâtis entre les choses et que je préfère aux choses, et surtout, loin des aseptiques images de la Mescaline, je reviens à mon grand mêloir, qui me rend plus ivre qu'elle ne le peut.
>
> Confluences incessantes de ruisselets venus de partout qui font la douceur des réservoirs 'santé', vrai infini, que leur extrême variété seule empêche de trouver infini.
>
> Et je reviens à mes forces. Qui l'eût cru? Mes forces! Avec quelle délectation adolescente je les sens revenir.
>
> Joie, joie pour la première fois aussi de ma vie, de me trouver de la volonté, de retrouver celle pour qui j'ai toujours été bien injuste (pas d'importance) mais où j'ai été bien peu perspicace. Ma grande découverte d'après la drogue: la volonté. Je la vois partout à présent, je m'en vois plein, en employant partout et là où je m'en doutais le moins. (*MM*, pp. 87–8)

In *Connaissance par les gouffres* the author writes: 'Une fameuse machine que l'homme! Jamais, jamais plus—me promettais-je—jamais plus je n'en dirai du mal. Ce serait trop sot, après tout ce que j'ai appris maintenant, sur ses pouvoirs prodigieux...' (*CG*, p. 155). And *Les grandes épreuves de l'esprit*, beginning with a piece pointedly entitled 'Le merveilleux normal', makes its exploratory intentions quite clear:

> Je voudrais dévoiler le 'normal', le méconnu, l'insoupçonné, l'incroyable, l'énorme normal. L'anormal me l'a fait connaître. Ce qui se passe, le nombre prodigieux d'opérations que dans l'heure la plus détendue, le plus ordinaire des hommes accomplit, ne s'en doutant guère. (*GE*, p. 9)

In the recent experimental period Michaux has widened his span enormously, probing the Infinite while delving back into the microscopic corners of the private psyche, dispersed into the universal Void but contracted attentively in his observation-posts, savouring transcendence and detachment but identified more than ever with the world of men. In the 1968–71 Addenda to *Misérable miracle* (1972), the poet stresses a dual achievement. On the one hand, thanks to this incredible 'Révélateur mental', a new depth and complexity of self-revelation: 'une nouvelle vigilance inconnue auparavant est là, installée, observatrice, réfléchisseuse' (*MM*, p. 173). On the other hand, and perhaps most important, his accession to a 'Conscience unificatrice, d'une telle amplitude qu'elle fait paraître ensuite le monde, dit réel, comme une altération du monde unifié' (*MM*, p. 177), and the realization, hitherto incomplete, of one's unity with the universal ensemble:

Partage à l'infini. Tout, interconnecté; tout et tous, échangeurs, ensemble.
Ensemble à perte de vue. (*MM*, p. 177)

There can be no doubt that the encounter with mescalin has been an enormous event, 'indiscutable, dépassant tout ce que j'ai connu, en tous sens géant', an event to which he has raised and adjusted himself almost superhumanly, 'pourtant à ma hauteur... à ma taille qui s'y proportionne' (*MM*, p. 174). Like his ductile Meidosems, he has stretched beyond his own reach to a new definition of himself.

IV

TECHNIQUES: HUMOUR AND EXORCISM

Among Michaux's many weapons of attack and defence, self-projection and withdrawal, a special place must be made for a technique which is both mental attitude and literary device: humour.[1] Humour is an all-purpose instrument, variable and versatile. It plays a game of perspectives, allowing one to see things in another light, from another angle, at a different distance. It enables one to disengage from the object of contemplation, to change its proportions and its pressures, to enjoy superiority where there was perhaps a threat of subordination. It disobeys the dictates of the ready-made. It gives the humorist a host of possible relationships with reality and with himself. It allows him to perform a balancing-act between reality and appearances, committed to neither.

The word 'clown' recurs in Michaux's writing. Perhaps he has been able to adopt it so readily because of his acute sense of his own inadequacy and ineptitude, an ineptitude which has left him no alternative but to make of it an art. Perhaps, too, his fluctuating position between a variety of contradictory selves, with none of which he feels any lasting identification, has given him an extraordinary sceptical detachment from himself and an inability to take himself seriously. Moreover, his natural remoteness from the superficial preoccupations of the world at large has made it easy for him to consider it as an absurd passing spectacle. For it is only one step from a phrase such as: 'Jamais je ne sentis que ses trous et d'où elle était absente' (*Ec*, p. 84), to the sense of a false and derisory décor, and to the kind of laughter of which one could say: 'Pareil au fou rire de certains aliénés, il exprime particulièrement la prodigieuse absurdité de tout' (*CG*, p. 25). One of Michaux's earliest texts 'Fils de morne' tells of a whole populace afflicted, much to the astonishment of the King, by a dreadful malady: the loss of expression. The first to suffer, of course, are the professional writers; but the clowns, whose language is one of signs, contortions and comic mimicry, manage to make the most of the disaster:

Des hommes sont directement frappés dans leur métier, tant mieux, je parle pour les écrivains, plus crissants que la craie, enfin disparus. Mais pauvres clowns. Enfin ils ne sont pas à un métier près, et tout le monde sait que le plus infime des clowns possède une occupation objective, si l'on peut dire, et des qualités acrobatiques qui ont leur utilité. (*Q JF*, p. 81)

The choice of the phrase 'occupation objective' is significant: the clown's mode of expression is not direct self-revelation or second personal address, but a screen of comic play and distortion standing between him and his public. He 'objectifies' himself through humour. He literally turns himself into an object, throwing himself into the arena in third personal form for public consumption. In the same work (*Q JF*, p. 51) the author writes: 'Les clowns n'ont pas de père; aucun clown n'a de père; cela ne serait pas possible', implying, among other things, that the clown is a kind of bastard in the world who has only an unnatural and adopted relationship with life. But the poem entitled 'Clown' (*ED*, pp. 249–50) proposes the most complex web of suggestion. Here, instead of the poet heaping petty indignities on his presiding 'Roi' who becomes a figure of fun, he knocks *himself* about with a grim derision and cuts himself down to size: 'CLOWN, abattant dans la risée, dans le grotesque, dans l'esclaffement, le sens que contre toute lumière je m'étais fait de mon importance'. Throughout the poem there is emphasis on a gymnastic dissociation from all that constitutes the artifice of his everyday, social self and the false dignity and self-respect which go with it. Rimbaud said contemptuously, 'tant d'*égoïstes* se proclament auteurs':[2] Michaux is not afraid to sacrifice the *moi* and, in so doing, to exorcize it. As he topples himself and falls about, he is 'Réduit à une humilité de catastrophe'; 'Ramené au-dessous de toute mesure à mon rang réel, au rang infime que je ne sais quelle idée-ambition m'avait fait déserter'; and 'Anéanti quant à la hauteur, quant à l'estime'. (At the same time he can look back with pitying amusement and appreciative irony at the unaltered pompousness of his fellow-men: 'mes semblables, si dignes, si dignes, mes semblables'.) As he becomes crystallized in the objectivity of the one word 'CLOWN', the *je* virtually disappears from the poem as a source of tension. 'Vidé de l'abcès d'être quelqu'un', the poet finds the relief of anonymity. 'Perdu en un endroit lointain (ou même pas), sans nom, sans identité', he savours the salvation of that translation elsewhere which is the comic. As he says in *Connaissance par les gouffres* (p. 25): 'Le rire fait abandonner des positions de trop de contrainte'. This is not the only time that Michaux abstracts himself from an unacceptable situation and his own personality by altering his proportions: whether he reduces himself to inflammable matchstick or diminutive clown, or whether he is inflated to megalomaniacal stature so that he can say: 'Je suis l'empereur de la planète Saturne' (*Q JF*, p. 49), in each case he is transforming himself into objective myth and relieving himself of the torments of an inconclusive intermediate existence.

Another circus-image becomes relevant here: the man shot from the cannon into a safety-net. At the moment of most extreme tension and contradiction, during the German occupation, Michaux speaks of 'laughing up another sleeve' and of his 'laughing-gun', a sombre gun detonated by fear and frustration, not aiming back at the Germans but projecting his spirit out of their grasp and keeping it intact:

> Je ris, je ris tout seul dans une autre
> dans une autre
> dans une autre barbe
>
> Je ris, j'ai le canon qui rit
> le corps canonné
> je, j'ai, j'suis
>
> ailleurs!
> ailleurs!
> ailleurs!
>
> (*EE*, pp. 11–12)

Jean Cayrol, writing of an 'univers concentrationnaire' which can no longer be exorcized by 'blanches paroles', refers to all the 'défenses surnaturelles de l'homme'.[3] Among these he includes 'rêves concentrationnaires' or 'rêves lazaréens'. He calls these dreams, and one could add to their list humour, distracting fictions and eccentricities of the imagination, a kind of private Resistance movement: 'les rêves devenaient un moyen de sauvegarde, une sorte de 'maquis' du monde réel dans lequel l'homme était à jamais fidèle aux reflets, même les plus étranges, de sa destinée et de sa continuité'.[4] Michaux's humour performs just such a function. The explosion of laughter, thrown in the face of reality, is the liberation of the spirit of the prisoner and the guarantee of its invulnerability. As he says on one occasion when mescalin is threatening to exercise its absurd dictatorship: 'Un rire énorme, que je ne pouvais trouver, m'eût peut-être libéré' (*CG*, p. 86). Frequently it draws on the energy of despair. An important passage 'Les Craquements' (*EE*, pp. 25–6) tells how, at the end of his childhood, he became bogged down in marshy ground and heard barking sounds all around, the minatory gestures of a reality eager to devour a life with no foothold: a voice advised him to hold them at bay by barking in return, but he found himself impotent. Years later, he attained firmer ground and was now assailed by cracking noises, presumably the sign of the continued fragility of the structure of his life: the answer might have been to respond in kind, to counter cracking with cracking, but it is not a noise the pliabilities of the flesh can make. Sobbing, similarly, was out of the question now that he was on the verge of manhood. For twenty years the cracking and barking continued unabated; he found no effective counter-measure or source of relief; the situation, it seemed, was an impasse. It was then that he discovered the containing power of laughter, a painful expedient to be sustained *ad infinitum* for fear that the slightest lapse would let in again the agents of destruction: 'Alors je me mis à rire, car je n'avais plus d'espoir et tous les aboiements étaient dans mon rire et aussi beaucoup de craquements. Ainsi, quoique désespéré, j'étais également satisfait'. Indeed, laughter and pain are never far removed from each other in Michaux. The poem 'Glu et gli' (*Q JF*, p. 61) indicates that, however vague their respective spheres of reference, they are close companions:

> le rire est dans ma...
> un pleur est dans mon...

And the poet's laughter is, in essence, a protective wall of lies: 'Sa façade de rires et de nerfs était grande, mais elle mentait. Son ornière était tortueuse. Ses soucis étaient ses vrais enfants' (*EE*, p. 51).

Plume, whom we have already compared with Charlie Chaplin, is Michaux's most notable tragi-comic clown. He represents a crucial development in the author's work: 'Avec *Plume*, je commence à écrire en faisant autre chose que de décrire *mon* malaise. Un personnage me vient. Je m'amuse de mon mal sur lui' (Bréchon, p. 205). Michaux gives a more elaborate description of the character's function when he calls him a 'personnage-tampon', a buffer-character, comparable in value with his imaginary countries or 'Etats-tampons' and such tribes as the 'Emanglons' and the 'Hivinizikis': 'En voyage, où presque tout me heurte, ce sont eux qui prennent les heurts, dont j'arrive alors, moi, à voir le comique, à m'amuser' (*Pass*, p. 154). Plume stands as a protective double between him and reality, turning the inadequacies of one and the threats and hard edges of the other into a safe comic confrontation, a spectacle from which the author himself stays detached: 'Dès que j'avais trouvé un personnage (que j'avais "reculé" en lui), j'étais tiré d'embarras, de souffrance (du moins du plus gros, du plus intolérable)'. In the same way the 'Mages' of Michaux's *Au Pays de la Magie*, by their intriguing activities, their unfortunate accidents, their mystifying attitude, and their ironic oscillations between the sublime and the ridiculous, kept him so well separated from the Brazilians (a race to whom he felt singularly maladjusted) during an actual journey to South America 'que je pourrais presque dire, malgré le temps passé là-bas, que je n'en ai pas rencontré' (*Pass*, p. 155). The idea of a 'recul' is important. In words as applicable to his own humour and its *dédoublement* as to the state of the schizophrenic which he is describing, Michaux says: 'En parlant, il fausse compagnie. Il est à distance...S'agissant de lui-même, il répugne à dire "je". Il ne dit plus "moi", il dit "celui-ci", il dit "lui". Distance' (*CG*, p. 262). It is humour applied consciously or unconsciously as a system of defence. When under the encroaching influence of psilocybine, part of him feels the need to retreat from the actual battlefront and take up new positions behind the lines:

Dans l'épreuve psilocybienne qui m'amoindrissait, je prenais du recul, je me mettais en état de défense, reportant mes défenses vers l'arrière d'une façon inconsciente. Ce fut une surprise pour moi, à relire mon texte, d'y trouver tout au long de l'ironie, signe d'une vigilance d'infirme prêt à un combat d'arrière-garde. (*CG*, p. 53)

The humour of imagination itself deserves particular mention. At one level, there is the oddity and incongruity of dream which, placing man in a strange *tête-à-tête* with his figurative forms, allows him to watch himself as if he were a foreign body: 'Le rêve qui paraît drôle provient de ce que l'homme se parlant à lui-même cesse de se gêner' (*Q JF*, p. 16). Michaux has always felt himself full of private madmen, eccentrics and *inadaptés* of all kinds who have no voice in the world of normality: 'Ah! par exemple, y en a-t-il de pauvres fous en moi!' he complains in *Qui je fus* (p. 18); and yet he realizes that to leave these without expression is, from the literary point of view, to reduce oneself to silence: 'Qui cache son fou, meurt sans voix' (*FV*, p. 65). Dream liberates them to their extravagances, lets them play truant and *faire le fou*. At the same time it liberates the author from the grip of their frustrated underworld. At another level, there is the realm of inventive fantasy in which the poet indulges his spirit of play: 'L'imagination, tout l'intéresse. Tout la pique, aussitôt amusée à broder, fabuler, placer et déplacer' (*CG*, p. 25). Here, he can juggle with reality for his own entertainment, fashion myths and fictions without constraint, and watch the antics of his creation with a quasi-divine immunity. As he once said of himself, in disparaging terms which do less than justice to the import of his imaginative activity: 'Oh! je n'ai rien de l'explorateur, je me promène seulement, je tire des billes de ma poche et je joue' (*Q JF*, p. 28). The imaginary countries of *Ailleurs* are the most advanced example in the author's work of this 'game of marbles', but he applies a more sophisticated metaphor: they are the expression, he says, of 'la soif de transformer, de refaire, de dépasser, *de canonner les atomes...*' (*Aill*, p. 8).

Michaux's humour has an enormous range of tones and styles. There is the gently disengaging satire of *Un Barbare en Asie*, slightly offhand and flippant, which allows the traveller to sum up the Hindus or the Malays in a quick entertaining sketch and pass on, always available for the next experience; or the absurd satirical exposé of 'Le Secret de la situation politique' (*FV*, pp. 85–9), more Voltairean in spirit, where, in a style of absolute order and clarity which only succeeds in sowing total confusion, the author introduces us to the political relations of the 'Ouménés de Bonnada' with the neighbouring 'Nippos de Pommédé', with the 'Nibbonis de Bonnaris' and so on, then to the various internal factions within the 'Ouménés de Bonnada' (the 'Dohommédés de Bonnada', the 'Odobommédés de Bonnada', the 'Orodommédés de Bonnada', the 'Dovoboddémonédés de Bonnada'), until, by a *reductio ad absurdum*, we are obliged to abandon to their futility all the divisions and sub-divisions, opinions and counter-opinions, of the government and diplomacy of nations. There is the pantomime of 'Villes mouvantes' (*QJF*, pp. 38–46) where we witness the inept gesturing of stock characters all at sea in a simple symbolic fable; or the knock-about farce of 'Mon Roi' (*LNR*, pp. 13–19) where the King is booted up the behind, covered with kitchen refuse, pelted with crockery and stuffed to the ears with foul-mouthed insults. There are Michaux's challenging sarcasms, found frequently in the essays of *Passages*, which take the dormant 'hypocrite lecteur' by the ears; or his mystifying proverbs and maxims, laconic capsules such as: 'Qui sait raser le rasoir saura effacer la gomme' (*FV*, p. 60) and: 'Le sage trouve l'édredon dans la dalle' (*FV*, p. 79), pseudo-philosophical 'boules hermétiques' within which the author keeps his own soft interior protected while toying with the reader and sending him off on a possible wild goose chase. There is the sadistic humour of 'Le grand combat' (*QJF*, pp. 74–5) where, with a vengeful relish and a derisory use of language, the poet works out his hidden frustrations and turns himself into *bourreau* extraordinary; or the black comedy of many parts of *La Nuit remue*, where the most macabre details are reported in a casual 'throw-away' manner, with a grating clash of tones, a false naïveté or accompanied by a pathetically out of place apology or understatement.

Liberté d'action (1945), where humour and the exercise of mental magic are seen as one and the same process, offers a particularly characteristic illustration. 'Les Envies satisfaites' (*VP*, pp. 12–13) records the therapeutic effects of his 'mental' murders, inflicted on odious specimens not just once but innumerable times and performed as a spectacle 'avec le soin et le désintéressement voulu, (sans lequel il n'est pas d'art) et avec les corrections et les répétitions convenables'. The humour which pervades the whole piece, and is itself a performance of 'désintéressement voulu', stems from its strange mixture of malice and naïveté, ferocity and formality, which upsets moral perspectives: the quaint outrage of a man (more sinned against than sinning) who complains that murders committed in real life always seem to cause you trouble afterwards: 'Et c'est le comble, venant de morts et pour la mort desquels on s'est donné tant de mal'; the decorous, gentlemanly expression of a polite narrator who, having just smashed a person's 'gueule abhorrée' into his shoulders, can calmly say: 'si un détail m'a gêné, je le relève séance tenante et le rassassine avec les retouches appropriées'; the final half-reassuring, half-undermining *envoi* of a writer who turns himself playfully into a character, a sort of mock-Bluebeard or bogeyman, saying (with an unsettling emphasis on 'presque' and 'sans doute'): 'Mon cœur vidé périodiquement de sa méchanceté s'ouvre à la bonté et l'on pourrait presque me confier une fillette quelques heures. Il ne lui arriverait sans doute rien de fâcheux. Qui sait? elle me quitterait même à regret...'. In 'La Cave aux saucissons' (*VP*, pp. 14–15) the narrator pounds important social personages into sausages and stores them in his cellar, savouring the spectacle of rank and dignity toppled from its perch, drawing comic relief, in both senses, from the discrepancy between pretention and reality (even though this reality is only his illusion), and prospering in his own cathartic high spirits, his 'instinct infaillible de jubilation'. In other texts he casts himself as the unimpeachable public moralist: in an untrustworthy atmosphere of potential aggression and sadism, he adopts a suave, patronizing tone with his readers, indulges in cool self-congratulation and offers finger-wagging moral advice. He takes pleasure in little tongue-in-cheek, self-dramatizing conclusions, in the vein of: 'Heureusement que nous ne nous rencontrons pas' (*VP*, p. 37) or: 'Je l'excuse, mais qu'il fasse attention' (*VP*, p. 41), which leave him, not a spent force, but still poised in potential over the end of his passages like an impending justicer. And throughout the collection he flits with perfect aplomb between illusion and reality, drawing the consequences of one into the other with an entertaining innocence, no longer the victim of their arbitrary divisions and contradictions.

In the broadest sense, all the forms of Michaux's humour, as well as his dream-sequences, controlled or spontaneous, are an act of exorcism. In the Preface to *Épreuves, exorcismes,* however, the author gives a more specific definition of the word. He sees the general function of poetic exorcism as that of eliminating the many incompatibilities and disharmonies produced within the self, like so many foreign bodies, by the accidents of events, and of releasing the individual from the network of dependences and subserviences inflicted by reality. For this reason he describes it as 'le véritable poème du prisonnier', the aim of which is to 'tenir en échec les puissances environnantes du monde hostile'. But he makes an important distinction between exorcism proper and what he calls 'exorcisme par ruse', a stratagem expressing itself largely in 'Rêves' and 'Rêves éveillés': involuntary subconscious dreams and deliberately elaborated artistic day-dreams. The former effect their exorcism 'Par ruse de la nature subconsciente qui se défend par une élaboration imaginative appropriée'; and the latter 'Par ruse concertée ou tâtonnante, cherchant son point d'application optimus'. It is indeed such 'exorcismes par ruse' which constitute the main body of Michaux's own work. Despite a similarity of intention and effect, however, the inventive and ingenious manoeuvres of 'Rêves' and 'Rêves éveillés' cannot be confused with the act of pure exorcism illustrated in the first few poems of *Epreuves, exorcismes*:

Effet libérateur pareil, mais nature parfaitement différente.

Rien là de cet élan en flèche, fougueux et comme supra-humain de l'exorcisme. Rien de cette sorte de tourelle de bombardement qui se forme à ces moments où l'objet à refouler, rendu comme électriquement présent, est magiquement combattu.

Cette montée verticale et explosive est un des grands moments de l'existence. On ne saurait assez en conseiller l'exercice à ceux qui vivent malgré eux en dépendance malheureuse. Mais la mise en marche du moteur est difficile, le presque-désespoir seul y arrive.

Michaux expands his definition of the process in a remarkably precise way:

L'exorcisme, réaction en force, en attaque de bélier, est le véritable poème du prisonnier.

Dans le lieu même de la souffrance et de l'idée fixe, on introduit une exaltation telle, une si magnifique violence, unies au martèlement des mots, que le mal progressivement dissous est remplacé par une boule aérienne et démoniaque—état merveilleux!

Unlike many of the poet's earlier forms of magic, it works its spell by violence rather than restraint, a reckless energy rather than prudent control, heat of passion rather than anaesthesia, and by hurling itself into head-on confrontation with the object of opposition rather than by retreating or setting it at a distance as a safe spectacle. But the effects—liberation, the elimination of suffering, the annulment of the enemy, and the isolation of the poet within the immunity of the 'boule'—are the same. The poem 'Année maudite' embodies most of these features:

Année
année maudite

année collée
année-nausée
année qui en est quatre
qui en est cinq
année qui sera bientôt toute notre vie...

Année, la narine au vent
mais rien ne vient

Souffrance
sur ta coque vide!

Anxiété
sur ta coque vide!

Famine
sur ta coque vide!

Année, année, année
que nous ânonnons sans fin,
compagnons de la cendre
des débris calcinés
poursuivi de plis
poursuivi de plaies...

                    (*EE*, pp. 18–19)

Here, one can feel words used as a battering-ram, thumping away insistently at the walls of a year which refuses to give way; or one can picture the poet in his bomb-turret, holding this hideous war-year obsessively in his sights as a target and shattering its cohesion with wave after wave of explosive verbal matter. There is a very definite 'martèlement des mots': words like 'Souffrance', 'Anxiété', 'Famine' are hammered out in a single blow and leave the shell of the 'année maudite' vibrating after the shock. A 'magnifique violence' grows rapidly into a state of 'exaltation': as the repetitions gain ground, the ternary rhythms impose their influence and spontaneous word-play creates its liberal links, one senses the poet generating his own intoxication which will, in turn, dissolve 'le mal' and seal him in the euphoria of his 'boule aérienne'. One senses, too, the efficacy of a black magic ritual ('boule aérienne et *démoniaque*') or an act of malediction. The 'élan en flèche, fougueux' and 'montée verticale' are more apparent, on the other hand, in the opening sequence of 'Lazare, tu dors?' where individual words shoot from each other like the different stages of a rocket and the poet, launched from the word 'Guerre', flies higher and wider into a 'stratosphere' of association:

> Guerre de nerfs
> de Terre
> de rang
> de race
> de ruines
> de fer
> de laquais
> de cocardes
> de vent
> de vent
> de vent
> de traces d'air, de mer, de faux
> de frontières, de misères qui s'emmêlent...
>
> (*EE*, pp. 15–16)

The technique of exorcism has continued to have repercussions in Michaux's writing beyond the war-poems of *Epreuves, exorcismes*. The terms he uses in a 1950 essay (*Pass*, pp. 159–64) to characterize the workings of 'malediction' indicate that it is a process very close to that already encountered. The belligerent vocabulary is maintained. He speaks of a charge of *surhaine* launching itself in an all-out offensive, the aim of which, however, is not so much destruction as the creation of a powerful motor within the self: 'Non blesser ou supprimer l'adversaire, mais par l'opposition à l'adversaire, créer en soi le Dragon de feu'. Again, a superhuman impetus, speed and rhythm are seen as the means of volatilizing matter and transporting the poet into a kind of levitational world apart:

> Grâce au rythme, le mouvement enlève le plus grave de la matière; son poids, sa résistance.
> Vitesse, soulagement du mal, du bas, du lourd. Sorte d'antimatière, d'idéal au premier degré.

He refers especially to the beneficial effects of 'les malédictions en chaîne' (a description well applicable to the style of the earlier 'Année maudite'), the reading of which proves almost invariably, he claims, to be intensely tonic. His concluding words strike a familiar note: 'la magie de malédiction, elle est, avant tout, martèlement, martèlement, martèlement'. Similarly, the 'action-poems' of *Poésie pour pouvoir* (1949), and in particular 'Je rame' and 'A travers mers et déserts' (*FV*, pp. 25–31), are described as 'deux attaques, qu'on appela poèmes, deux poèmes appuyés', dependent once more on that 'Utilisation *énergétique* de l'ennemi, de la situation irritante, du milieu hostile, du mal' and fulfilling in a new context the function of a 'bélier de guerre' (*Pass*, pp. 207–11).

V

STYLE AND STRUCTURE

'J'étais une parole qui tentait d'avancer à la vitesse de la pensée' (*Q JF*, p. 22): one of the most remarkable characteristics of Michaux's style is its speed. It is a rapid, dissatisfied style, in constant pursuit of thoughts, mental communications, rhythmical invitations, images and impulses which are formed and re-formed almost before words can move. He has elasticated and accelerated the poetic instrument to an extraordinary degree, the resultant poem being not a literary arrival but the record of an inconclusive *trajet*. Lines from *Un Barbare en Asie* summarizing the essence of different oriental languages give an indication of what Michaux's own style is and is *not*. Hindustani words, on the one hand, fill him with contempt:

> Béats avec une bonasserie paysanne et lente, énormément de voyelles bien épaisses, des â, et ô, avec une sorte de vibration ronflée et lourde, ou contemplativement traînarde et dégoûtée, des î et surtout des ê, une lettre d'un niais! un vrai bê de vache. Le tout enveloppé, écœurant, confortable, eunuchoïde, satisfait, dépourvu du sens du ridicule. (*BA*, p. 19)

His own expression, by contrast, is highly charged and tensile, restless and uncomfortable, angular and aggressive, rhythmically agitated, contemplatively avid, and enlivened by a sense of ridicule which not only pushes the world away and rebelliously alters its features, but turns inwards to shatter any sluggish identification with the self and set up a field of force between the poles of the parted personality. Arabic, on the other hand, is born of a spirit close to his own. It is in movement to-and-fro. In written form, it is like the flight of an arrow, or many arrows, across the page:

> Son écriture est une flèche... L'écriture arabe, elle, n'est qu'un trajet, une ligne faite de lignes. Dans l'écriture ornée, elle va toutes flèches bien droites, que de temps à autre un accent traverse et sabre. Cette écriture, véritable sténographie, est quatre fois plus rapide que l'écriture latine. (*BA*, p. 49)

So, in Michaux, one meets a telegrammatic style, spasmodic and elliptical. There is his 'Télégramme de Dakar' (*Pl*, pp. 94–6), tapped out vehemently, desperately, like a distress signal; or his 'Ecriture d'épargne' (*VP*, pp. 121–2) which looses five penetrating shafts in swift succession to compose the following startling self-portrait: *speed*

> Foreuse
> Perceuse
> habitacle de sel
> dedans une tourterelle
> Hérisson de frissons.

There are, more recently, his dynamic drug-texts. One, entitled 'Tapis roulant en marche', is an effort to keep up with the racing impertinence, the levitational iconoclastic games of a hashish-inspired vision. Words leap to life, breathlessly passing the baton to other words in an endless relay, spanning great gaps of the inexplicable, in an invigorating movement of *maladresse* and *élan* (see *BA*, p. 40):

> Soudain, précipice.
> En bouillonnant
> une eau torrentielle cascade dans le fond d'un cañon
> vive, vive, vivacissime.
>
> Tenant fortement un grand anneau métallique
> je serre, je serre
>
> Je...pensée, voyons, c'était avant
> mais quelle était donc cette pensée?
>
> 'Paolo! Paolo!'
> crié d'une voix bordée de rouge
>
> Oublis
> oublis à grande vitesse...

(CG, pp. 93–4)

Another, describing his acceptance of the flood of mescalin, shows language, carried on impulsive ternary rhythms, constantly over-stepping itself, partially erasing and re-writing, never satisfied with the first impression, adding, correcting, overlaying:

Moi-même j'étais torrent, j'étais noyé, j'étais navigation. Ma salle de la constitution, ma salle des ambassadeurs, ma salle des cadeaux et des échanges où je fais entrer l'étranger pour un premier examen, j'avais

perdu toutes mes salles avec mes serviteurs. J'étais seul, tumultueuse-
ment secoué comme un fil crasseux dans une lessive énergique. Je
brillais, je me brisais, je criais jusqu'au bout du monde. Je frissonnais.
Mon frissonnement était un aboiement. J'avançais, je dévalais, je
plongeais dans la transparence, je vivais cristallinement. (*MM*, pp. 48-9)

There could be no better or more varied illustrations, one diffuse,
the other compact, of what he calls elsewhere 'Allégresse de la
vie motrice' (*FV*, p. 18).

It is a style characterized by proliferation and multiplicity.
Just as he feels a kinship with the equatorial forest, where one is
ill at ease in a burgeoning tangle of life-forms, so Michaux favours
expression which is a thicket of interrelated images, all surging
to life irrepressibly, competing and intermingling:

> partout jaillissement
> carrefours de jaillissements
> geysérisation.
>> (*CG*, p. 101)

Its movements are 'mouvements à jets multiples' (*FV*, p. 15). Its
agents provocateurs come not single spies but in batallions. In this
way, a poem like 'Emportez-moi' (*LNR*, p. 182), which begins
in deceptively familiar terms reminiscent of Baudelaire's 'Moesta
et errabunda' or even Mallarmé's 'Brise marine', rapidly develops
into a dense conglomeration of complementary or alternative
images which seem to breed indefatigably. As the regular
decasyllabic lines of the opening make way for a less predictable
rhythm and the theme of departure in time and space acquires
more and more unusual facets, one's interpretative sense is
jostled by a variety of suggestions within the same experience:
the desire to be in the forefront of some thrusting motive force
or dispersed in its wake; to be absorbed into a smoothly textured
but untrustworthy pure surface which can give way and pull
one downwards; to be carried in a confluence of airy breaths or
become part of a weightless spent force; to be an easy traveller
both in outer and inner space, transported not only outwards into
the air but into the inner rhythms and lines of communication of
the body; to be simultaneously eliminated yet precariously
preserved and intact. The floating final line, with its surprising
adjustment, is particularly influential in leaving the poem
balanced between different directions, journeys in the horizontal

plane or descent into the vertical; while the last ambiguous verb might represent a negative self-burial or integration into the secret life of *la profondeur*:

> Emportez-moi dans une caravelle,
> Dans une vieille et douce caravelle,
> Dans l'étrave, ou si l'on veut, dans l'écume,
> Et perdez-moi, au loin, au loin.
>
> Dans l'attelage d'un autre âge.
> Dans le velours trompeur de la neige.
> Dans l'haleine de quelques chiens réunis.
> Dans la troupe exténuée des feuilles mortes.
>
> Emportez-moi, sans me briser, dans les baisers,
> Dans les poitrines qui se soulèvent et respirent,
> Sur les tapis des paumes et leur sourire,
> Dans les corridors des os longs, et des articulations.
>
> Emportez-moi, ou plutôt enfouissez-moi.

Michaux's texts do not reduce the world to unity and stability. They explore a wish, an impulse, a moment's extraordinary perception, a vibration in all their passing complexity, contradiction and effervescence. They try to make themselves the equal of a play of forces which always runs beyond them and tears open any attempt to circumscribe. Consequently their structure is never a simple linear one, nor do they reach a neatly rounded conclusion. As he says of the theatre of Southern India: 'Il y a là-dedans une force qui fouette et dit: "Allons, ne traînez pas, n'arrondissez pas" ' (*BA*, p. 122). The forms of many of his most characteristic poems are governed by

> Mouvements d'écartèlement et d'exaspération intérieure plus que mouvements de la marche
> mouvements d'explosion, de refus, d'étirement en tous sens. (*FV*, p. 14)

Their rapidly moving configurations do not propose a clear meaning and direction but are

> Signes de la débandade, de la poursuite et de l'emportement des poussées antagonistes, aberrantes, dissymétriques. (*FV*, p. 19)

They represent an unresolved moment of inner tensions, disruptive influences, deviant temptations. It is a multi-directional

poetry. Certain texts express themselves as 'lacets innombrables'
(*CG*, p. 119) overlapping or intertwining with other 'lacets';
others set up vertiginous swirling motions particularly influential
on this poet who describes himself as 'fort sensible au tournoie-
ment' (*Pass*, p. 9). Others may be seen to develop, like the sway
of ether, in 'saccades en escalier qui durent quelques secondes'
(*LNR*, p. 76): in short-lived successive spasms rising one over the
other and rendering each previous one, if not irrelevant, then
relative and expendable. In almost all, coherence and unity are
threatened, not only by 'des images nocives, images à faire
tomber' (*CG*, p. 114) which dislodge the imagination and send it
reaching over great expanses which logic cannot bridge, but by
the encroachments of space and void: 'Ecarts agrandis en ravins'
(*CG*, p. 114) and 'Des mondes de vide entre les mots' (*CG*, p. 119).

   Despite the disjunctive form and embattled atmosphere, however, Michaux's poetry shows itself extraordinarily sensitive to
the idea of a continuum. His early observations on oriental
art-forms provide a revealing commentary on his own in this
respect. Chinese music, which he finds especially cathartic, has a
curious dual quality, for, while full of explosive effects and jarring
interruptions, it is bathed in an overall melodic continuity which
creates a sense of peace:

Ce qui gêne surtout les Européens, c'est l'orchestre fait de fracas, qui
souligne et interrompt la mélodie. Cela, c'est proprement chinois. Comme
le goût des pétards et des détonations. Il faut s'y habituer. D'ailleurs,
chose curieuse, malgré ce formidable bruit, la musique chinoise est tout
ce qu'il y a de plus pacifique, pas endormie, pas lente, mais pacifique.
(*BA*, p. 152)

Not only the title, but also the movement and structure, of the
author's *Paix dans les brisements* become more meaningful in
relation to these comments: one could even speak of 'Brisements
dans la paix', a play of fragmentation and shattered particles
contained and redeemed within the peace-bearing flow of
repetitive rhythms and patterns. A description of a Cingalese
cinema performance is even more illustrative. Explaining how
the showing of an old Western film, full of fast-moving episodes
and incident, in fact gave him no sense of agitation, he says:

Cela pour une raison étonnamment simple, c'est que le film était
accompagné du pouls constant de formidables coups de tam-tam, pan,

pan, pan, pan, pan, qu'essayaient de traverser les sons religieux d'un harmonium.

Aucun autre film ne m'a donné cette impression d'éternité, du rythme sans fin, du mouvement perpétuel.

On s'agitait stupidement pourtant dans ce film. N'empêche, ce film était fixe. Il était emporté par plus immense que lui, comme une cage de coqs lutteurs dans un train express. (*BA*, pp. 133–4)

The image of a cage of fighting cocks inside an express train, of antagonism and flying fragments within a smoothness of movement which transcends them, of wildly changing directions within a single imperturbable progression, of a variety of tempos subordinate and relative to another overriding tempo, is particularly appropriate to Michaux's work, and especially to the recent long poems of the mescalin and post-mescalin period. Yet another recollection from the Asian journeys of the early 1930s confirms the influence of this pattern, perhaps unconscious, in the poet's nature. Again it is a question of discontinuity, disharmony and a criss-cross of violent lines of force held within the cadences and vaster rhythmical fabric of a continuum, an interplay creating a constant impression of extension into a beyond:

Le plus beau mouvement théâtral que je vis, fut à un *théâtre malais de Singapour*. Des pêcheurs armés de couteaux et de fascines de roseaux luttaient contre des sortes de poissons-scies. La lutte était formidable. Cependant si incroyablement scandée, que les infiniment divers mouvements paraissaient tissés dans quelque mécanique et appartenir à un autre monde. (*BA*, p. 226)

One thinks of an *infini turbulent* carried and finding its salvation within an even greater *infini*. Michaux's mescalin experiences have certainly allowed him to explore this latent structure with new significance, emphasizing on the one hand the restless, disruptive motions of the drug, 'Demonstratrice du discontinu' (*IT*, p. 12) and on the other the all-absorbing, all-containing universal flow of

> le poème interminable
> le poème aux vers idéalement beaux
> sans rimes, sans musique, sans mots
> qui sans cesse scande l'Univers
> (*IT*, p. 82)

with which it has a secret relationship.

Repetition is a vital structural element in Michaux's poetry. The universal poem apprehended through mescalin is described as 'litanie, litanie de la Vérité' (*IT*, p. 82), and elsewhere he expresses his susceptibility to this ideal: 'revenir, revenir à la même chose, être litanie, litanie comme la vie, être longtemps avant de finir' (*Pass*, pp. 133–4). He speaks of the mysterious virtues of monotony and repetition ('Il y a dans la monotonie une vertu bien méconnue, la répétition d'une chose vaut n'importe quelle variété de choses, elle a une grandeur très spéciale'), and takes the example of the attraction of the sea, which is 'la répétition d'un peu d'eau, la répétition considérable' (*Ec*, pp. 190–2). It is an attraction closely linked to the tendency towards intoxication: 'Il y a dans ma nature une forte propension à l'ivresse' (*Ec*, p. 169), he writes. The poem 'Dans la nuit' (*ED*, p. 104) is a fine illustration of the 'intoxicant' use of sound, syntax and structure. It is a contemplative chant, inducing a kind of union between himself and the limitless body of the night as, like the sea, it extends its rippling sameness and continuity into the furthermost points of the universe. Mallarmé's words: 'En se laissant aller à le murmurer plusieurs fois on éprouve une sensation assez cabalistique',[1] apply to it perfectly. A trance-like effect and the sense of being invaded by a vast uniformity are produced by the unrelieved repetition of word, sound and rhythm (the all-pervasive assonance of *i*, the numerous internal rhymes and approximate echoes, the switch rhymes such as 'nuit...uni' and 'Et fumes...Et mugis', the little phonetic chain-reactions such as 'Sa plage boit, son poids est roi, et tout ploie'). And yet one notes that there are subtle variations within the deceptive monotony. The two isolated end-stopped lines, which stand out against the overall fluency and mark points of transition ('Mienne, belle, mienne' and 'Nuit qui gît, Nuit implacable'), subtly accentuate the theme of possession or non-possession; the change to a second person address in the central section, framed between a third personal introduction and finale, gives an unobtrusive intimacy coinciding with suggestions of fertility and fullness; and, despite the harping recurrence of the word 'nuit', one is rolled gently among a variety of properties of night, swirling together to form what Baudelaire, in his 'Correspondances', calls 'une ténébreuse et profonde unité':

Dans la nuit
Dans la nuit
Je me suis uni à la nuit
A la nuit sans limites
A la nuit.
Mienne, belle, mienne.
Nuit
Nuit de naissance
Qui m'emplis de mon cri
De mes épis
Toi qui m'envahis
Qui fais houle houle
Qui fais houle tout autour
Et fumes, es fort dense
Et mugis
Es la nuit.
Nuit qui gît, Nuit implacable.
Et sa fanfare, et sa plage,
Sa plage en haut, sa plage partout,
Sa plage boit, son poids est roi, et tout ploie sous lui
Sous lui, sous plus ténu qu'un fil,
Sous la nuit
La Nuit.

At other times repetition is used to drum up will-power and create a condensation of force, as in *Poésie pour pouvoir*:

Je rame
Je rame
Je rame contre ta vie
Je rame
(*FV*, p. 27)

or it may create a feeling of exaltation by a more expansive quasi-Biblical rhetorical period:

On a bavé sur ta progéniture
On a bavé sur le rire de ta fillette
On est passé en bavant devant le visage de ta demeure.
(*FV*, p. 27)

It may reinforce an act of revolt, or, as a concert of 'Tams-tams morbides' (*Pl*, p. 95), provide the ritual framework for a poetic malediction or black mass. It may act as a recurrent rhythmical life-line to which one resurfaces after being plunged persistently into a maelstrom of centrifugal and conflicting imagery, as in 'Dans le cercle brisant de la jeune magicienne' (*FV*, pp. 241–2). It may set up cyclic or numerical patterns to suggest some mysterious or magical order. Or, perhaps more frequently, it is the expression of some kinetic force projected violently outwards from the self, only to return in a looping, agitated course and be re-projected: 'boomerang qui sans cesse revient' (*FV*, p. 17).

Michaux is a unique master of the poem with no other formal framework than an emphatic rhythmical contour, a predilection borne out by the title of one of his latest works, *Par la voie des rythmes* (Fata morgana, 1974) which, dispensing with words themselves, is nothing but a complex of visual signs formed into rhythmical movements. His interest in the resources of different rhythms is as apparent in the travel-journal of *Un Barbare en Asie*, where he is fascinated by the singing and cymbal-playing of a group of Civa worshippers executed 'dans un rythme rapide et diabolique, un damné chant de sorcellerie qui vous prenait irrésistiblement' (*BA*, p. 89); as in the essays of *Passages*, where he says of music: 'Le rythme à lui seul suffit pour vous faire "marcher" et danser, cependant que les timbres qui résonnent vous soumettent à un ébranlement confus né de vibrations' (*Pass*, p. 193); or as in the mescalin texts, where he speaks of underlying dislocating rhythms active within the context of wider ones saying: 'Mais je n'ai pas assez dit l'importance omniprésente et sous-jacente des rythmes' (*IT*, p. 102). 'Clown' (*ED*, pp. 249–50) exemplifies a typical rhythmical structure in Michaux's verse:

Un jour.

Un jour, bientôt peut-être.

Un jour j'arracherai l'ancre qui tient mon navire loin des mers.

Avec la sorte de courage qu'il faut pour être rien et rien que rien, je lâcherai ce qui paraissait m'être indissolublement proche.

Je le trancherai, je le renverserai, je le romprai, je le ferai dégringoler.

D'un coup dégorgeant ma misérable pudeur, mes misérables combinaisons et enchaînements 'de fil en aiguille'.

Vidé de l'abcès d'être quelqu'un, je boirai à nouveau l'espace nourricier.

A coups de ridicules, de déchéances (qu'est-ce que la déchéance?), par éclatement, par vide, par une totale dissipation-dérision-purgation, j'expulserai de moi la forme qu'on croyait si bien attachée, composée, coordonnée, assortie à mon entourage et à mes semblables, si dignes, si dignes, mes semblables.

Réduit à une humilité de catastrophe, à un nivellement parfait comme
après une intense trouille.
Ramené au-dessous de toute mesure à mon rang réel, au rang infime
que je ne sais quelle idée-ambition m'avait fait déserter.
Anéanti quant à la hauteur, quant à l'estime.
Perdu en un endroit lointain (ou même pas), sans nom, sans identité.
CLOWN, abattant dans la risée, dans le grotesque, dans l'esclaffement,
le sens que contre toute lumière je m'étais fait de mon importance.
Je plongerai.
Sans bourse dans l'infini-esprit sous-jacent ouvert à tous,
ouvert moi-même à une nouvelle et incroyable rosée
à force d'être nul
et ras...
et risible...

The poem has small beginnings. But the phrases rapidly gather
impetus and swell. The more or less remote promise ('Un jour. /
Un jour, bientôt peut-être') soon becomes imminence, and,
though expressing a future wish, the relentless volley of verbs
becomes a present act of volition: the wishful is superseded by the
active, the brief and verbless by the profuse and energetic. As
the repetitions intensify, there is a kind of fever and intoxication
by rhythm which is a forerunner to that loss of sterile self-
ownership which is a major theme of the poem. Applying one of
the central images of the poem, one could see the development of
the first half as a succession of 'mini-abscesses', each building up
and then drained in turn by a violent or definitive verb. The
initial: 'Un jour' expands and becomes more pressing in: 'Un
jour, bientôt...', before flowing out more emphatically in the
unpunctuated: 'Un jour j'arracherai...'. The second movement:
'pour être rien et rien que rien, je lâcherai...' follows a similar
course: a triple repetition, more vehemently contracted, which
eventually finds release in the rhyming verb and the long sibilant
alliteration which extends in its wake. This makes way for another
verbal pressure-point, throbbing and acute ('Je le trancherai, je
le renverserai, je le rompraI, je le ferai dégringoler'): a sequence
of three violently active verbs (the ternary rhythm seeming to
act as a magic formula in this exercise of self-liberation) finally
broken in form by the infinitive structure of the fourth which
transfers part of the energy from the inside to an outside agent.
The tone swells again with the forceful self-derision of: 'ma

misérable pudeur, mes misérables combinaisons…', in an incomplete sentence which, compressing together heavily worked alliterations and cumbersome multi-syllabic vocabulary, is not grammatically relieved until the separate next paragraph. This opening movement finally reaches its 'bottleneck', a peak of constipation and tension, a central segment clogged with double, triple and quadruple repetitive forms, a monstrous composite noun ('dissipation-dérision-purgation'), a bracketed question which can only be wedged in as a hasty aside, and a jostling collection of multi-syllabic abstract words. An accumulation of energy stage by stage; an almost uncontainable 'blockage' of pulsing verbal matter; followed by a silent explosion and a progressive self-dispersion: such is the structure of 'Clown'. From this point on, the poem seems suddenly alleviated. One would say that its initial motivating force had burst. The second half consists of verbless fragments falling downwards one after the other ('Réduit…Ramené…Anéanti…Perdu'): as past participial phrases, they have little independent energy and change the mood in a flash from active to passive. Placed at the head of their phrases, they induce a downward intonation. The volitional impetus of the future tenses is lost and so, more significantly, is the emphatic 'je' which governed them. In this region of experience which is 'sans nom, sans identité', the self, too, becomes 'other', conceivable only in the impersonality of metaphor ('CLOWN') and therefore partially metamorphosed. In the final lines (which, like the first, are verbless, so that the central act of poetry swells out of the non-activity of idealism and finally subsides into the non-activity of fulfilment), the movement of descent is continued almost to disappearance and wordlessness. Devoid of capitals and unemphatic, they have no spirit of initiative. The last few words, left hanging in the air, suggest absence as much as presence: loosely linked by the feebly repeated 'et', they are little more than a weak ripple. They are, moreover, vague adjectives: qualities without substance. Together with the 'je', nouns and verbs are left behind, and it becomes a poem without matter or resistance, without body or energy: a poem with 'nobody'. One thinks back to Michaux's definition of poetic exorcism: 'Dans le lieu même de la souffrance et de l'idée fixe, on introduit une exaltation telle, une si magnifique violence, unies au martèlement des mots, que le mal progressivement

dissous est remplacé par une boule aérienne' (*EE*, pp. 7–8).
'Clown' passes through these stages: from pain (that of frustration) and obsession, through a feverish excitement, violence and
verbal incantation, to a dissolution and ultimate airiness or
acceptance into space. Its structure can be seen as a movement of
rhythmic ascent and downfall ('qu'est-ce que la déchéance?'), or
as a 'concentration du moi' followed by a 'vaporisation du moi'.
Its course could be plotted on a graph (or perhaps more appro-
priately on an electro-encephalogram) as a steeply rising line
more and more wildly disturbed by a close succession of forceful
impulses, until it reaches a crisis-point, and finally relapses in a
series of spacious and increasingly gentle vibrations. It could be
seen equally as a poem 'entre centre et absence': it grows from
almost nothing and finally disappears into almost nothing. It is
interesting that a similar structural pattern governs the early
poem 'L'Avenir' (*LNR*, pp. 199–200). This poem, too, grows
from the seed of a distant promise, then expands and proliferates
violently, using repetitive rhythms and intoxication by sound.
The build-up of its opening lines can be compared with that of
'Clown':

> Quand les mah,
> Quand les mah,
> Les marécages,
> Les malédictions,
> Quand les mahahahahas,
> Les mahahaborras,
> Les mahahamaladihahas,
> Les matratrimatratrihahas...

Ultimately, after a most gymnastic use of language, a thick
accumulation of imagery and an almost unbearable tension, this
poem, too, seems to burst open and fades away in an alleviated
and airy finale:

> Plus jamais.
> Oh! vide!
> Oh! Espace! Espace non stratifié... Oh! Espace, Espace!

The conclusion suggests that a certain charge of poetic energy
has been expended. It is, one might say, a 'suicidal' conclusion:
like that of the South American Indian's flute-music which, after
a pattern of stretched and searching three-note repetitions,

'retombe, et va à cette note profonde qui en est la fin, ou plutôt le suicide, ou encore le mortel épuisement. L'eau ouverte où il fallait sombrer' (*Ec*, p. 185).

One cannot hope, in a study of these proportions, to give more than a glimpse of the dynamics of a style which is not a static artistic feature but a live reponse. Some of Michaux's texts are accelerated. Others are slowed down. Some are disseminated and in movement. Others, like 'Icebergs' (*LNR*, p. 93), are dense and stilled. Some are fluid and expansive. Others are sharp and elliptical. Some are 'streams'. Others, like the aphorisms of 'Tranches de savoir' (*FV*, pp. 37–83) and the recent *Poteaux d'angle* (Edns. de l'Herne, 1971), are 'pebbles'—reminiscent once again of the Arabic model in which the author appreciates 'une espèce de tension, un mot juste, une situation lapidaire...Brèves sentences, bref éclat' (*BA*, p. 50), and even more so of the style of Lao Tzu of which he says: 'Rien n'approche du style de Lao-Tzeu. Lao-Tzeu vous lance un gros caillou. Puis il s'en va. Après il vous jette encore un caillou, puis il repart' (*BA*, pp. 186–7). Above all, some of his texts are short or long poems in approximate verse form. Others, composing the backbone of his work, are highly diverse passages of prose: the lucid, crisply narrative and matter-of-fact dream-accounts of *La Nuit remue* which, with their sudden twists of direction and inconsequential pseudo-conclusions, throw one off balance while pretending to reassure; the highly imaged, chastened blocks of *Meidosems*, whose hidden laws of alternation and interplay prick out the most subtle structural designs; or the taut progressive sequences of 'L'Etranger parle' and *L'Espace aux ombres*, the forms and arrangement of which are governed by the pulsations of some occult field of force. All of these can only be signalled as avenues for exploration which critics have so far preferred to leave off their route.

VI

POETRY AND PAINTING

Michaux has never been the natural ally of words. Their respective interests are not easily compatible. Verbal language is stiff and slow-moving, laden with convention and association, riveted to rationalism and the need to signify, devoted to ordered, nameable things and congealed within a limited circle of meanings as soon as it touches the paper. It cannot do justice to the multi-dimensional, evasive flux of mental reality. In *Ecuador* the poet sees the act of writing, which is the imprisonment of the errant and unlimited within a fixed form, as a death, saying: 'Je n'ai écrit que ce peu qui précède et déjà je tue ce voyage' (*Ec*, p. 11) and: 'Il y a quelques minutes j'étais large. Mais écrire, écrire: tuer, quoi' (*Ec*, p. 16). Broaching a problem which becomes increasingly acute in the mescalin experiments, he describes how the state of chastity (abstinence and self-deprivation) acts like a drug on him, producing enriched mental movements, accentuated emotions and fluidity of awareness; but it is in such moments, frustratingly, that words give only the most skimpy summary and show themselves to be a clumsy cripple: 'Si j'écris dans ces moments, impossible, ce n'est jamais qu'un résumé. Pourtant, hélas, c'est mon optimum lucide' (*Ec*, p. 105). Similarly, in *Passages* (p. 31), he speaks of all that shifts below the surface of words like an obscure submarine life, 'véritables bancs d'idées, nombreux à en avoir la respiration coupée, mais d'un délicat, d'un flou, d'un tel en deçà des mots-pensées!' and referring to these multiple organic life-forms drifting at various oceanic levels as his secret 'plankton', he expresses his contempt for the superficial verbal realm which, pretending to give account of it, is its inevitable betrayer: 'Mots, mots qui viennent expliquer, commenter, ravaler, rendre plausible, raisonnable, réel, mots, prose comme le chacal' (*Pass*, p. 132).

It is not therefore surprising that Michaux should seek some other mode of expression more appropriate to the underlying complexity and mobility of experience. The opening sentence of *Emergences, résurgences* gives a neat summary of one of his major reasons for adopting painting as his second language:

Né, élevé, instruit dans un milieu et une culture uniquement du 'verbal'

je peins *pour me déconditionner*. (*ER*, p. 9)

In this, the adventure of painting is hardly different from those physical journeys undertaken in 1929–30 which he calls 'voyages d'expatriation', intended to shake off the habits of an acquired culture and the monocular vision which it imposes. Breaking from the dictatorship of words, it allows him to start again from scratch in a medium less heavy with ancestors and allegiances, to re-discover the world through new eyes, to manipulate it from a different distance and through different tentacles. It is one of those 'other lives' mentioned in the Postface to *Plume* (p. 213), in which one is less afflicted and paralysed by deprived sub-conscious selves. It is a means of correcting an imbalance in his personality, for 'L'écriture comme seul pilier, c'était le déséqui-libre' (*ER*, p. 19). The 1938 essay 'Peindre' (*Pass*, pp. 83–5) speaks excitedly of painting as an inner voyage, a switch to another network of lines of distribution and a kind of rebirth:

Le déplacement des activités créatrices est un des plus étranges voyages en soi qu'on puisse faire.

Etrange décongestion, mise en sommeil d'une partie de la tête, la parlante, l'écrivante (partie, non, système de connexion plutôt). On change de gare de triage quand on se met à peindre.

La fabrique à mots (mots-pensées, mots-images, mots-émotions, mots-motricité) disparaît, se noie vertigineusement et si simplement. Elle n'y est plus...

Etrange émotion. On retrouve le monde par une autre fenêtre. Comme un enfant, il faut apprendre à marcher. On ne sait rien. On bourdonne de questions. On essaie constamment de deviner...de prévoir...

Nouvelles difficultés. Nouvelles tentations.

Tout art a sa tentation propre et ses cadeaux.

The 'gifts' or rewards of painting prove, for Michaux, to be particularly precious. It is a direct, immediate language, corres-ponding in a more meaningful way than writing to an ideal which, unobtainable or not, lingers with him: 'Le désir, l'appel et le mirage d'une vraie langue directe subsistent en moi malgré tout' (*FF*, p. 39). When his boat first touches South America in 1928, he has the intuition that a painter could do more with this unprecedented encounter than a man searching for words. For, while the writer, confronted with the formless matter of a reality which refuses labelled compartments, pursues it vainly with nouns and ready-made connotations, the painter catches nameless things spontaneously as outline, colour and texture before they are actually even objects. One of Michaux's 'Tranches de savoir' describes a different encounter: that of the racing shadow of a panther playing across the fur of a fleeing deer, a shadow deepening in the penultimate split second before the animal pounces and takes its prey. Who, he asks, has ever had the leisure to observe and record such a moment? 'Seul un peintre (assez bon tireur pour ne pas tirer prématurément ni perdre la tête et l'occasion de cette délectation si rare), seul un peintre et particulièrement sensuel en ombres, peut avoir fait l'observation désirée, dans un esprit d'abandon, de rigueur et de plénitude convenable' (*FV*, p. 50). It is interesting that the painter's art is seen here as that of a 'bon tireur', a carefully aimed and detonated projectile capable of hitting at speed, not simply a moving target, but a play of impalpables, two different tempos, two kinetic forces, caught on convergent paths in a fatal momentary relationship. If it makes its move a fraction too late, all it has on its hands is a death-scene. The final words of *Liberté d'Action*, a work which would seem to represent a triumph of psychic and verbal magic, are: 'D'ailleurs je ne tue plus. Tout lasse. Encore une époque de ma vie de finie. Maintenant, je vais peindre, c'est beau les couleurs, quand ça sort du tube, et parfois encore quelque temps après. C'est comme du sang' (*VP*, p. 46). Here, the death-process of literary exorcisms, willed and deliberate, is exchanged for the immediacy, the surging unselfconscious life-source of painting. Clearly, its value is not in the end-product or after-effects, but in the motive act itself. The original inspiration and final form hardly matter, but simply the unleashed energy and speed of what takes place in between and acts as a kind of transport. As Michaux says of his early 'Dessins commentés' (*LNR*, p. 40), painting is not concerned with being its own analyst or investigator: 'un dessin ne s'ausculte pas'. It represents a re-discovery of spontaneity. The laborious 'word-factory' is brought to a halt, and he plunges into an expansive *laisser aller* where he finds himself 'dans le désordre, dans la discordance et le gâchis, le mal et le sens dessus dessous, sans malice, sans retour en arrière, sans reprise, innocemment' (*ER*, p. 39). A painting, for Michaux, is an *œuvre ouverte*: not so much a process of doing as of undoing, and its aim not so much to resolve as to release. In a crisis of feeling, he snatches up a blank sheet, falsely virginal and removed from reality, and proceeds to disfigure it, spoliate it, turn it into an open wound:

> L'humeur sombre, je commence, en ayant attrapé une, à fourrer dessus quelques obscures couleurs, à y projeter au hasard, en boudant, de l'eau, par giclées, non pour faire quelque chose de spécial, ni surtout pas un tableau. Je n'ai rien à faire, je n'ai qu'à défaire. D'un monde de choses confuses, contradictoires, j'ai à me défaire. (*ER*, pp. 35–6)

He speaks of the paper as a place of clash, encroachment, metamorphosis and destruction, where nothing is left intact, identities are negated and definitions dissolved:

> Je lance l'eau à l'assaut des pigments, qui se défont, se contredisent, s'intensifient ou tournent en leur contraire, bafouant les formes et les lignes esquissées, et cette destruction, moquerie de toute fixité, de tout dessin, est sœur et frère de mon état qui ne voit plus rien tenir debout. (*ER*, pp. 40–1)

No painting, moreover, has any final or ultimate value. Each is part of the dispensable and disposable matter of his inner dynamics; each is swallowed in a whirlwind of appearance and disappearance, creation and destruction, discovery and loss:

> Dans une pièce prêtée, entourée d'arbres...je couvre de dessins des feuilles de papier. Puis je les déchire. J'en refais. A l'aventure. Je les déchire encore. Je les déchire. Conserver est vite agaçant.
>
> Mon plaisir est de faire venir, de faire apparaître, puis faire disparaître. (*ER*, p. 21)

Michaux repeatedly stresses the values of painting as speed and movement, peculiarly appropriate to turning a status quo into a revolution, a blockage into a liberation, a prison into a horizon. 'Je suis de ceux', he writes, 'qui aiment le mouvement, le mouvement qui rompt l'inertie, qui embrouille les lignes, qui défait les alignements, me débarrasse des constructions. Mouvement, comme désobéissance, comme remaniement' (*ER*, p. 65). It is the medium in which he becomes most easily sheer *élan*. It allows him to communicate, without artifice or impediment, with his deepest inner tempos. It espouses the sinuous, fluctuating contours of reality and lends itself to the rhythms of the universal continuum. It is for this reason that Michaux turns to the graphic arts in order to 'Dessiner l'écoulement du temps', saying:

> Au lieu d'une vision à l'exclusion des autres, j'eusse voulu dessiner les moments qui bout à bout font la vie, donner à voir la phrase intérieure, la phrase sans mots, corde qui indéfiniment se déroule sinueuse et, dans l'intime, accompagne tout ce qui se présente du dehors comme du dedans... (*Pass*, p. 197)

and for the same reason that in a dream he opens, not a book, but a folder of the most expansive and vibrant gouaches and exclaims: 'Enfin je voyais, non plus l'esquisse fuyante, mais le monde comme je le conçois dans son étalement prolifique' (*Pass*, p. 104). Not only does painting, free from the restrictive practices of words, rejoin the primitive and the primordial but it opens itself to a totality of experience. This is as true for the creator as for the spectator:

> Les livres sont ennuyeux à lire. Pas de libre circulation. On est invité à suivre. Le chemin est tracé, unique.
> Tout différent le tableau: immédiat, total. A gauche, aussi, à droite, en profondeur, à volonté.
> Pas de trajet, mille trajets, et les pauses ne sont pas indiquées. Dès qu'on le désire, le tableau à nouveau, entier. Dans un instant, tout est là. (*Pass*, p. 115)

Here one can begin to read some of the 'mille trajets' of Michaux's own paintings, a language to which he was converted, at the age of twenty-six, by the discovery of Klee, then Max Ernst and Chirico. He saw in it, even then, the revolutionary possibility of undermining the terms of his life, an instrument of his desire to expose the illusory nature of the so-called real world:

> La peinture tout à coup à vingt-six ans me parut propre à saper mon état et mon univers.
> En même temps je tenais à montrer du monde concret son peu de réalité. (*ER*, p. 116)

But it is not until 1937, the year of his first exhibition at the Galerie Pierre in Paris, that he can say with any firmness: 'Commence à dessiner autrement que de loin en loin' (Bréchon, p. 21). By this time the complex influence of Oriental art has come to join and probably outweigh that of Klee or the Surrealists. Chinese painting holds a particularly deep message for him.

Despite the fact that it is mainly concerned with landscape, it
evades the actual substance of things and initiates one to a hidden
life of line and movement: 'Le mouvement des choses est indiqué,
non leur épaisseur, et leur poids, mais leur linéarité si l'on peut
dire' (*BA*, p. 158). It devotes itself to signs. It satisfies in Michaux
the desire for space and dimension, for incompleteness and
suggestive absence, for light, flitting movement and sudden
impetus:

> Mais c'est la peinture chinoise qui entre en moi en profondeur, me
> convertit. Dès que je la vois, je suis acquis définitivement au monde des
> signes et des lignes.
>
> Les lointains préférés au proche, la poésie de l'incomplétude préférée
> au compte rendu, à la copie.
>
> Les traits lancés, voltigeants, comme saisis par le mouvement d'une
> inspiration soudaine et non pas tracés prosaïquement, laborieusement,
> exhaustivement façon fonctionnaires, voilà qui me parlait, me prenait,
> m'emportait.
>
> La peinture, cette fois, sa cause était gagnée. (*ER*, p. 16)

 Michaux's first urge to draw and, as he puts it, to participate
in the world through drawing expressed itself in lines: lines in
movement, lines with their own appetite, roaming, inquisitive
lines. He lets each one run within the available space on the
paper, seeking its own form and purpose, expending all its energy
for adventure, until it is forced to curl back on itself or trail away
into loss. The result is: 'Un emmêlement, ce qu'on voit alors, un
dessin comme désireux de rentrer en lui-même' (*ER*, p. 11). Like
the Meidosem, it is something which has no centre or fixed form,
but which cannot be disunited or extricated from itself; something
obliged by space or sheer exhaustion to relinquish its movements,
but remaining infinite, without beginning or end. It is a tangle
of quest and self-containment, an exploratory *boule*. It is an
adventurer and a Narcissus, a line interfering with itself, breaking
its own outline, with no exterior object by which to direct its
movements, and yet unwilling to relapse into that self-enclosed
unity which gives things a false resolution and brings them to an
untimely end: 'se traversant elle-même sans broncher, sans se
détourner, sans se nouer, sans à rien se nouer' (*ER*, p. 12). It
circumscribes nothing, and is itself uncircumscribed: 'Sans rien
cerner, jamais cernée' (*ER*, p. 12). It is 'entre centre et absence'.
It moves in that enigmatic 'en dedans-en dehors qu'est le vrai

espace' (*FV*, p. 190). Tracing its patterns between two poles or in a field of force where it fluctuates to a host of attractions but submits to none, it escapes that 'loi de domination-subordination' (*FV*, p. 185) which habitually plagues Michaux's poetic world. It neither dominates nor is dominated: 'Ni dominante, ni accompagnatrice, surtout pas subordonnée' (*ER*, p. 13). It is *disponible*. It is a wayward celibate line, engaging and disengaging, not yet ready for a false marriage. The poet's imaginative essay on Paul Klee (1954) is entitled 'Aventures de lignes' (*Pass*, pp. 173–80). Here, he is fascinated by the living network of lines: lines on the move, 'Les voyageuses, celles qui font non pas tant des objets que des trajets, des parcours'; lines not complete in themselves but always on the verge of exploration; lines sprouting, spiralling, drawn into a proliferating cellular expanse; lines which delve beneath the surface and do their work underground, not concerned with facial features but with some secret focus inside the head; lines divorced from substance and volume which are 'lignes-signes, tracé de la poésie, rendant le plus lourd léger'; lines meeting other lines and departing, in a play of convergence and divergence, attraction and repulsion; lines which like his own 'ligne somnambule' (*ER*, p. 12) float in the fluid world of dream ('On n'avait jusque-là jamais laissé rêver une ligne', he says of Klee) and which, advancing for the sheer joy of advancing, refuse to arrive. The adventure of lines has not ceased to exercise its spell on Michaux. Through mescalin, for example, he rediscovers it with a new intensity: on the one hand, the jagged, spasmodic lines of *l'infini turbulent* which electrify the nerves and slash across the field of vision; on the other hand, lines of a different kind not adequately explored: 'Lignes religieuses, signe d'une phase *idéalisante*, sinon mystique' (*IT*, p. 169). And in his latest major collection, *Moments* (1973), a poem entitled 'Lignes' (pp. 27–31) celebrates legions of lines traced aimlessly on to the paper as an act of purification ('Ennoblie par une trace d'encre, une ligne fine, une ligne, où plus rien ne pue'), an act of liberation ('Echappées des prisons reçues en héritage, venues non pour définir, mais pour indéfinir'), an act of personal expansion and multiplication ('Dévalantes, zigzagantes, plongeantes pour rêveusement, pour distraitement, pour multiplement...en désirs qui s'étirent'), and as an abolition of finite boundaries and the sense of belonging:

D'aucune langue, l'écriture—
Sans appartenance, sans filiation
Lignes, seulement lignes.

No less compulsive than the sign-language of lines are the innumerable faces which loom from Michaux's sheets:

Dessinez sans intention particulière, griffonnez machinalement, il apparaît presque toujours sur le papier des visages.
Menant une excessive vie faciale, on est aussi dans une perpétuelle fièvre de visages. (*Pass*, p. 87)

They are untamed, ill-formed faces from some unknown source, perhaps 'faces of prey' unleashed by others, perhaps his latent inner men eager to find an outlet: 'Derrière le visage aux traits immobiles, déserté, devenu simple masque, un autre visage supérieurement mobile bouillonne, se contracte, mijote dans un insupportable paroxysme' (*Pass*, p. 88). They may be the tenacious faces of stifled or sacrificed personalities which have not received their due, of remote childhood fears, of unfulfilled desires and questing appetites, of that infinitely plastic and malleable second self which is silently shaped and re-shaped at every moment of the day behind the wall of one's actual thoughts and formulated expressions. In some way or other, they are all 'doubles'. They respond to Michaux's desire to depict, not external features, but 'un certain fantôme intérieur qu'il faudrait pouvoir peindre' (*Pass*, p. 92), 'un être fluidique' which lives apart from flesh and bones. So, in painting the colours of the double, red will not necessarily go on the cheeks or lips but to the region of a fierce inner fire; and the brush will follow the barometric readings of deep emotions which never appear as more than a faint flicker on the actual physiognomy. His aim is to explore mental and not geometrical perspectives: *l'espace du dedans* and its patterns of radiation. Michaux's pictorial faces are a startling example of what he calls *fantômisme*. They are visitations not fully fledged, defiant of unity, finality and significance. 'C'est tout traversé, partagé, dissous et dissolvant, un visage' (*ER*, p. 116), he writes. There are heads like death's heads, shot through with holes, confirming the poet's statement 'Je suis né troué' (*Ec*, p. 98); heads with no visible means of support, tilted at an unsure angle, of indeterminate composition, porous, dinted, mutilated, with the features obscured or half-erased by conflicting lines; heads with a double lurking behind them, the two soldered like Siamese twins yet at variance, with a 'je ne sais quoi, qui nous unit, tragique, et nous sépare' (*Pl*, p. 91); heads which are a mesh of electric wires, a mass of uncertain fissures and sutures, a minefield of detonating spots and craters; faces eyeing the void with tenacity, groping in the obscurity, grimacing with anguish; faces wistfully bovine, brutishly primeval, threatening to dissolve back into the unnameable whence they came. Their looks are distress-signals, 'S.O.S. lancés dans l'espace par des milliers de malheureux en détresse' (*ED*, p. 248), literally calls to 'save our souls'. In the words of Jean Cayrol: 'Nous traversons une période *sournoise* de la peinture contemporaine où tout peut arriver, se dégénérer, s'altérer sans que le peintre sache quelle main conduit son pinceau, quel regard épouvanté saisit sa vision sans rachat'.[1] As he paints, the portrait assumes a demanding life of its own: the paper may drink too quickly, an unintentional blob may form, his brush may make a false move, and through such accidents a face will infiltrate. The final portrait, for Michaux, is 'un compromis entre les lignes de forces de la tête du dessinateur et la tête du dessiné' (*Pass*, pp. 99–100), the result of a combat in which certain *trajets* are reinforced, others deflected and others cancelled out before the *trajet définitif*, the lines of a new disturbing face, are attained. Such faces are part of a monstrous self-investigation to which painting is more appropriate than words. For this reason Michaux says in 1945 (*Pass*, p. 67) that one can rely as much on painters as on geneticians for a wealth of experimental forms, and that painting is the drosophila of the artist: the most extensive means of sounding one's obscure heredity, larval forms and frightening mutations.

Michaux's painting does not wallow in a world of colours. Black is its dominant. In 1938 he writes: 'Pour le moment je peins sur des fonds noirs, hermétiquement noirs. Le noir seul est ma boule de cristal. Du noir seul, je vois de la vie sortir' (*Pass*, p. 85). The emergence of his faces is also associated with the colour black: 'Du pinceau et tant bien que mal, en taches noires, voilà qu'ils s'écoulent: ils se libèrent' (*Pass*, p. 88). Black is a primeval genetic source, where one must delve for the secret of human origins and the elucidation of one's own mystery. Black is the well of the most fundamental human instincts and emotions: 'De la nuit vient l'inexpliqué, le non-détaillé, le non-rattaché à des causes visibles, l'attaque par surprise, le mystère, le religieux, la peur...et les monstres, ce qui sort du néant, non d'une mère' (*ER*, p. 26). But black has another major expression in Michaux's work: the black of his later ink-drawings. The difference here is that, instead of light or coloured forms emerging tentatively from a primeval black base, one finds black dynamically superimposed on the expressionless white sheet. Instead of reception, there is action; instead of submission, an exercise of will. In the first instance it is the will of the ink itself, a sovereign power, a black barbaric flow devouring all in its path: a malcontent, an absolutist, spilling through obstacles, refusing boundaries. Then it is the opposing will of the painter, roused to anger and impudence by the choleric humour and cavalier encroachment of the ink, compelled to intervene and defend his sense of frontiers: he urgently splits the spreading pools, scatters and undoes them in dramatic gestures in which his own disgust and exasperation are liberated. The final drawing is the record of a struggle between two wills: a battleground of ruptured pseudopods, of dispersed and regrouped forces, in which his own tensions and inner movements have been reified. Michaux's most remarkable work in China ink is *Mouvements* ('Le Point du jour', Gallimard, 1951). It is a suite of kinetic signs, developed in the style of ideograms but where intelligible thought-content is replaced by pure movement and rhythm. It is here that the artist comes closest to an ideal he expresses thus: 'enfin j'avais un dessin démodelé, uniquement en gestes et en élans, comme je le voulais' (*Pass*, p. 107). Through page after page, tense black knots stretch, leap and flail in the air, thickening, lengthening, bunching, receding, whipped by the winds of space, combed by invisible rhythms, insatiably metamorphic. Though lacking arms, legs and trunks, they still represent man: 'homme par sa dynamique intérieure, tordu, explosé, que je soumets (ou ressens soumis) à des torsions et des étirements, à des expansions en tous sens' or 'homme écartelé se ruant vers on ne sait quoi, pour on ne sait quoi, cinglé par on ne sait quoi' (*ER*, p. 50). Freeing him from his verbal paraphernalia, 'ces collants partenaires', they carry the artist into the exhilaration of a new life of movement, 'à un débrayage non encore connu, à une désincrustation, à une vie nouvelle ouverte, à une écriture inespérée, soulageante' (*Mouvements*, Postface).

Before turning finally to Michaux's 'mescalin period' and to adjust the impression that his work is exclusively black and white, one should add a note on his use of watercolours. Even here it is not so much the colours as the movements and rapid transitions, the decompositions and recompositions, the gobbling chain-reactions which attract him:

> Le 'flash', les couleurs qui filent comme des poissons sur la nappe d'eau où je les mets, voilà ce que j'aime dans l'aquarelle.
>
> Le petit tas colorant qui se désamoncelle en infimes particules, ces passages et non l'arrêt final, le tableau. En somme, c'est le cinéma que j'apprécie le plus dans la peinture. (*Pass*, p. 108)

The colours are only thrown there as bait or as developers (in the photographic sense) in order to tempt something bigger to the surface or bring out a hidden image. Michaux is a spirit of water: 'j'avais la mer en moi, la mer éternellement autour de moi' (*EE*, p. 121), he says. Watercolours feed this affinity. They dissolve straight lines, infiltrate everywhere, expand in all directions; they blur reality and identity and suck one into a kind of liquid vertigo: 'Eau de l'aquarelle, aussi immense qu'un lac, eau, démon-omnivore, rafleur d'îlots, faiseur de mirages, briseur de digues, débordeur de mondes...' (*Pass*, p. 110). In this respect gouaches, which enforce a greater 'fidelity' to oneself, do not suit him (though he is soon to modify this opinion as he discovers new possibilities—see *ER*, p. 71): 'La gouache résiste davantage à l'eau. Elle fait son petit mortier contre les évanescences qui la guettent. Elle tente de respecter les intentions de l'auteur, du respectable auteur!' (*Pass*, p. 111); and his dealings with oils, 'cet élément pâteux, collant' (*Pass*, p. 113), have continued to be abortive.

There is no doubt that hallucinogenic drugs have provided an exceptional stimulus for Michaux's paintings and drawings. Lines, faces, the battle of black and white, the drama of speed and movement, are relived in a new dimension. If there was ever an acute and mobile spectacle for a painter's inner eye, mescalin provides the switch: innumerable points of colour and vibration surging forward, gathering together, swept into patterns, creating a fabric which disappears into infinity; intricate, restless sections of a psychedelic tapestry stretching away to the end of the world. Caterpillar movements, zig-zags, parallels, symmetrical echoes, seething repetitive conglomerations are all caught and carried in an incontrovertible, unanimous rhythm. Space becomes 'un monde fuyant...où tout est à la fois et n'est pas, montre et ne montre pas, contient et ne contient pas, dessins de l'essentielle indétermination' (*ER*, p. 106). Time dissolves into 'la durée devenue élastique, soudain anormalement longue, toutes dimensions à présent flottantes, incertaines' (*ER*, p. 96). Fixity becomes flux: 'flux traversant indifféremment le plus dur comme le plus souple, flux comme ces particules cosmiques qui traversent la terre sans s'arrêter, sans même ralentir' (*ER*, p. 96). Never has Michaux's drawing been more sensitive to shocks, dislocations, fragmentations, wild transitions and hot pursuits. And never has it been more sensitive to a changeless universal order. His latest works forget the self and its private obsessions, its movements of rage and frustration. In their place are *gestes-mouvements* of another kind, representative of the essential motive structures of reality: 'Résumé graphique d'une situation d'ensemble, de la plus métaphysique' (*ER*, p. 102).

Painting certainly holds many more surprises in prospect for Michaux. But he is no more addicted to this second language than to that of words. What he says of drugs he says, too, of painting:

Autre menace de fixation: la peinture elle-même créant, bien connu des peintres, un état de besoin. Voilà qui mettrait fin à mes voyages soudains, à mes départs en coup de vent.

Gare à l'assujettissement! (*ER*, p. 20)

His trajectories must remain an act of revolt,

VII

AN EVALUATION

Michaux is remarkable, not simply as a poet of refusal (refusal of himself, of his own language, of foreign bodies, of the notion of reality, of restrictions on thought, desire and dream), but for the variety of means, ingeniously developed, through which he consummates this refusal: exercises of mind over matter, attacks of the will, motionless meditation, demoniacal enthusiasm, exploited obsessions. As he says, under a pseudonym: 'Par la volonté appuyée sur le souffle, par la pensée sans souffle, par ses démons, Tahavi a rejeté' (*VP*, p. 115). Michaux has fully accepted his rôle as outcast and displaced person, one of a disturbing breed, ill-adjusted and under-nourished, whom he describes as 'Maigres, impropres à la vie, creusés par la recherche, hommes de nulle part' (*EE*, p. 44). He has moved to live in a no man's land, 'lieu de rencontre du dehors et du dedans' (*CG*, p. 212), where limits are obscured, one is always under duress and expression itself is threatened. Despite a public image of him as an elaborate escapist, his *ailleurs* is not a protected retreat. It is a heavily bombarded outpost where the real tensions of human nature are forcibly confined and put to the test. Michaux has always viewed his life as risk. In a condemned area more turbulent than that inhabited by Gide, he has agreed to play out his contradictions to the full, to expose and explore all his latent possibilities.

For, together with the poet of refusal who clenches himself into a *boule hermétique* and struggles to exorcize the hostile powers of the outside world, there is the poet of acceptance, generously throwing himself open to all available experience—to the murky monsters of the subconscious, to the tauntings and temptations of the imagination, to the extravagant visions of supranormal perception—in the knowledge that 'Un être humain est toujours extrêmement en dessous de ce qu'il pourrait être' (*IT*, p. 229). Michaux imagines a plant 'qui croîtrait dans les lieux d'exaltation, seulement là, noueusement chez les intolérants et les fanatiques, pas du tout chez les indifférents et admirablement auprès de ceux qui aiment avec transport, auprès des jeunes imaginations ivres d'avenir' (*FV*, p. 166). His own writings are just such a plant, growing in places of exaltation and intensified desire, animated by potent saps, admirably shaped (like his *arbres des tropiques*) into fascinating, avid forms, and cultivated by a sheer love of experience and possibility. Michaux is very much a young imagination. He has stayed identified with the spirit of childhood, seeing the world through eyes which are 'riches d'étendue, de désert, grands de nescience' (*Pass*, p. 51), and shown an exceptional ability to sustain or renew his own virginity. He is intoxicated with the future: 'Pour moi, pas de paradis en arrière' (*CG*, p. 61), he says. He is interested in the present only inasmuch as one is responsible for its horizons. But words like *transport* and *ivres* should not disguise the fact that Michaux's work is the very reverse of *inconscience*. Few poets can have ever been so eagle-eyed and vigilant. 'Ma vie est une insomnie' (*Q.JF*, p. 37), he writes. In his sleepless *voyage au bout de la nuit*, while others slip into unconsciousness, he supervises every trick of the mind, every ghost, every pulse of the unknown, letting none dupe or take advantage of him. It is hard to conceive of a writer more given to hallucination, vision and fantasy in a manner so totally unillusioned and lucid. Indeed, he has made himself the conscience of a whole tradition of visionary poetry. And despite his fanciful interventions, transmutations and love of all that might be, his works of imagination are in no way remote from reality: 'Cet extravagant joue en pleine réalité. Cet imaginatif a toujours les pieds à terre' ('Portrait d'homme' in *L'Herne*, p. 337). A link between Michaux and Francis Ponge may not seem the most obvious one to make. And yet he has committed himself in his own fashion to an unshakeable *parti pris des choses*, so that he can say with every justification: 'Je suis pour les réalités, vrai campagnard, moi, indécrottablement près des choses' (*FV*, p. 205). Nor can one overestimate all that this poetic 'absentee' has done to reveal, not only the unspeakable depths of his own flesh and nerves, but the infinite variations and nuances, all the potential lives of the animal, vegetal and mineral realms with which man has secret associations.

In *Misérable miracle* (p. 64) one reads: 'La médiocre condition humaine, il faut la parcourir de bout en bout, sans fin, sans honte'. Michaux has scoured the cavern of human possibility more ruthlessly and completely than any other contemporary French poet. In so doing, he has discovered not so much its limitations and mediocrity as its inexhaustibility. Early and late essays in *Passages* show how his appetites in this respect have hardly changed over the years. In 'Idées de traverse' (1942) he tells how one of his first delights was to take a dictionary and contemplate, with no particular awareness of individual ideas or definitions, all those countless unfurling buds of human effort (finally blending into them some of his own obscure inner urges and leading an adventurous little crew of his own 'à travers l'infini moutonnement des possibles'):

> Etincelles du monde du dehors et du dedans, j'y contemple la multi-tude d'*être homme*, la vie aux infinies impressions et vouloir être, et j'observe que ce n'est pas en vain que le monde humain existe. Même je succombe bientôt à ces myriades d'orbites. (*Pass*, p. 23)

And in 'Chandelier', written since 1960, he describes a magic chandelier with which he could walk through life, conjuring lost presences to existence, seeing what has never been seen before, illuminating all the innumerable hidden variants of human origins and development: 'Magnifique! M'emparant d'autres cas, d'autres entourages, d'autres origines, je saisirais des lois. Je comprendrais! Merveilleuse méditation panoramique!' (*Pass*, p. 242). Michaux repeatedly stresses the endless keyboard of human possibility and man's infinite plasticity. 'Non! Pas question de paix', he writes, 'Nous sommes inépuisables en expériences' (*Pass*, p. 67). He himself is an untiring Proteus. He sees the problem of artistic creation as 'celui de la renaissance, de la perpétuelle renaissance, oiseau phénix renaissant périodique-ment, étonnamment, de ces cendres et de son vide' (*ER*, p. 45). He has set out to experience the world through a succession of borrowed or adopted consciousnesses, each wrenching him from the familiar terms of his own. He has moulded and remoulded himself according to the spasms of unformulated desires: 'Désir qui aboie dans le noir est la forme multiforme de cet être' (*FV*, p. 12). He has sounded the shocks and subterranean rumblings of his personality without ever arriving at a final definition of himself: 'Comme une aiguille sismographique mon attention la vie durant m'a parcouru sans me dessiner, m'a tâté sans me former' (*VP*, p. 237). His work is an epic of unfinished self-scrutiny. It is also an epic of instability, adaptation, experiment and change. What he says of himself at the time of his childhood reveries is no less true of the ever-youthful septuagenarian: 'Un véritable prodige en mouvements. Protée par les mouvements' (*Pass*, p. 200). The nomadic Michaux is still propagating new atmospheres, new desires, new modes of apprehension. He is still proving human nature to be an unfathomed mystery and giving it a future. In this sense, perhaps more so than Rimbaud, he could claim of the poet's rôle: 'Enormité devenant norme, absorbée par tous, il serait vraiment *un multiplicateur de progrès*'.[1] At the same time this work which seems so self-enclosed and idiosyncratic, is deeply committed to the interests of humanity at large. Michaux's statement in the Postface (1934) of *La Nuit remue* sounded at the time somewhat hollow: 'Ce livre, cette expérience donc qui semble toute venue de l'égoïsme, j'irais bien jusqu'à dire qu'elle est sociale'. Today, it rings true as never before.

Michaux's texts have been slow to gain a reading public. Perhaps in a sense they have still not gained one. Indeed, perhaps the author has been unwilling to encourage it. For, in a 1959 interview, he stated: 'Je peindrai de plus en plus et j'écrirai de moins en moins. Ou alors je n'écrirai plus que sous la forme de poèmes très difficiles à traverser pour les autres: je reviendrai, si vous voulez, à mes deux cents lecteurs'.[2] His earliest publications, often appearing in very limited editions, met with only cursory reviews in periodicals. *Un certain Plume* (1930), with its disconcerting 'dead-pan' humour, caused hardly a ripple; the depth and complexity of the reporting in *Un Barbare en Asie* (1933) went largely unappreciated; the originality of style and vision of *Voyage en Grande Garabagne* (1936) remained, and still remains, to be discovered. During these years, André Rolland de Renéville in the *Nouvelle Revue Française* was Michaux's only consistent torch-bearer. Even André Gide's *Découvrons Henri Michaux* (1941), influential though it may have been thanks to the patron's name and as the first *plaquette* wholly devoted to the poet, was little more than a loosely stitched anthology and fell into something of a war-time vacuum. Michaux's reputation, in fact, has been shaped in the post-war period. René Bertelé must be given the essential credit for the breakthrough: firstly with the thirteen pages accorded to Michaux in *Panorama de la jeune poésie française* (1942), then with an article in *Confluences* marking the important publication of *L'Espace du dedans* (1944), and above all

with his full length study *Henri Michaux* (1946), one of the first
and still one of the richest of the invaluable 'Poètes d'aujourd'hui'
series published by Seghers. Since 1946, there has been a swelling
stream of essays, now no longer one or two page notes on
individual titles as they appear but analyses of crucial themes:
guilt and liberty, possession and dispossession, the imaginary
voyage, cruelty, metamorphosis, exorcism, rational magic,
poetry as power, artificial paradises, the two infinites, movement,
the Narcissus myth and so on. And yet, despite the fact that he
commands a prominent place in almost all the major panoramas
and anthologies of twentieth century French literature, despite
the number of substantial critical books which have appeared on
him since Bréchon's window-opening *Michaux* in 1959, and despite
the award in 1965 of the Grand Prix National des Lettres (which
he refused), one cannot help feeling that he has been fragmented
more than most according to people's hobby-horses and sensitive
stomachs, thought of in slogans, and only half-read. For some,
he is the 'absurdist' in the vein of Kafka, Camus and Beckett; for
others, a visionary from the Augean stable of Lautréamont or
Artaud, a tormented and unkempt Surrealist image-spinner. For
some, he is a humorist having affinities with Edward Lear, Lewis
Carroll, or Chaplin; for others, a utopian like Swift or Samuel
Butler, or a stylist and moralist like Voltaire. For many readers in
England he tends to be identified with the two words *Plume* and
exorcisme. In America he has been adopted by sections of the
intelligentsia as a cousin of the drug-scene, the underground,
psychedelic culture and transcendentalism. Michaux is all of
these, and much more. He is the poet who has assumed more
magnanimously and comprehensively than any other the imaginative, linguistic, philosophical and scientific destiny of his own
age: *our* age. It is hoped that, in emphasizing this, the present
study will have added a few more to Michaux's 'two hundred
readers'.

VIII

POINTS OF VIEW

...une sorte de poésie mystérieuse, mais aussi un malaise indéfinissable se dégage bientôt de tout cela. Le malaise vient de la relation qui s'établit involontairement en notre esprit entre l'imaginaire et le réel. Et ce malaise, parfois, traversant la bouffonnerie, tourne à l'angoisse. Après tout, se dit-on, tout cela, qui n'existe pas, pourrait être; et tout ce que nous savons qui est pourrait bien ne pas avoir beaucoup plus de réalité. Ce qui se passe sur cette terre n'est pas, somme toute, beaucoup plus raisonnable que ce que Michaux nous peint. Il excelle à nous faire sentir intuitivement aussi bien l'étrangeté des choses naturelles que le naturel des choses étranges.

André Gide, *Découvrons Henri Michaux*, Gallimard, 1941, p. 41.

Une œuvre qui décourage les commentateurs, parce qu'ils ne savent trop par quel bout prendre ces livres étranges qui sont à la fois journaux intimes, reportages, récits, contes et poèmes, et parfois tout cela en même temps; où l'on passe, sans crier gare, de l'humour le plus aigu au lyrisme le plus nu, le plus déchirant; de la fantaisie la plus gratuite au réalisme le plus brutal; de la description de pays imaginaires à celle de pays bien réels (et on ne sait lesquels des deux sont les plus réels); du ton métaphysique à celui du monologue intérieur et de la maxime au poème épique —sans aucun égard pour les genres.

René Bertelé, *Henri Michaux*, 'Poètes d'aujourd'hui', Seghers, 1965, p. 15.

Inventeur de pays fabuleux, inventeur d'hommes pour les peupler, inventeur de mots pour peindre ces hommes, il semble qu'Henri Michaux s'évertue à suppléer par l'incantation au grand vide que fait le monde en lui quand il l'a tué.

André Rousseaux, *Littérature du XXe siècle*, quatrième série, Albin Michel, 1953, p. 85.

Etre un grand névropathe avec une magnifique santé de l'intelligence, voilà le don de Michaux, le secret de sa découverte, de ses démarches audacieuses et rusées dans les infra-univers et les supermondes. Nous entrons avec lui dans les songes d'un malade qui ne peut trouver le sommeil,—mais semble ne convoquer le cortège des monstres que par une reprise de santé, pour échapper au vertige de la Nuit, à la présence d'un Non-Etre plus étranger et plus effrayant encore que tous ces étrangers hallucinants qui aboient vers nous dans le noir...Voilà une sensibilité de mage et de fée constamment surexcitée et survoltée par une intelligence cynique, voyeuse, impitoyable.

Gabriel Bounoure, 'Le Darçana d'Henri Michaux', *La Nouvelle N.R.F.*, No. 53, 1957, pp. 875–6.

Acte de présence au monde, dévoilement de l'homme: telle est cette œuvre dont le pathétique, parfois, se dissimule sous l'apparence du gratuit et du fantasque, comme sa signification se dérobe sous l'étrangeté des monstres individuels. De même qu'il n'est ici aucune description objective, aucune évasion fictive qui ne nous aide à prendre conscience de la réalité, il n'est aucun phantasme, si singulier qu'il soit, où l'éternelle condition humaine n'affleure. Vision subjective d'un malade, d'un fiévreux, hanté d'obsessions qui ne valent que pour lui-même? On le croit souvent et c'est ainsi, avouons-le, que l'auteur considère son œuvre volontiers. Au fond de ces hantises singulières, comment ne pas discerner, cependant, une irrécusable *universalité*? Cet univers du malaise, de l'insatisfaction n'est-il pas celui de toute inquiétude métaphysique profonde? Cette flore, cette faune larvaire, répugnante, qui accable l'esprit de sa prolifération cancéreuse, comment ne pas reconnaître en elle la nature même qui nous entoure, à laquelle nul ordre rationnel n'a donné une forme qui convînt à l'esprit? Et l'être qui est au centre de tout cela, le héros du drame, cet être que tout blesse et que tout déçoit, à qui manque toujours quelque chose de décisif qu'il ne peut pas même nommer, cet 'être troué' qui ne sent en lui que vide et absence, accablé par la multiplicité infinie de la nature parce qu'il aspire à l'ordre et à l'unité, mais rassuré aussi par cette multiplicité parce qu'elle lui paraît un masque devant un vide plus terrifiant encore, cet être traqué à la fois par une absence obsédante et une présence excessive, comment ne pas s'écrier devant lui: *ecce homo*?

Gaëtan Picon, *Panorama de la nouvelle littérature française*, Gallimard, 1960, p. 226.

Ce qui rend Michaux si singulier, c'est autant que sa continuelle angoisse, son formidable humour. Il y a chez Michaux une ironie sans nom, et presque une allégresse de la férocité. S'il choque et ravit tant, c'est moins parce qu'il est brutal ou monstrueux que parce qu'il est aussi désarmant de naturel, à la fois sérieux et incongru, méchant et infiniment tendre. Michaux est tout de rage et d'abandon, et rien n'échappe à la lucidité mordante et dérisoire, rien, si ce n'est une sorte de grande bienveillance qu'on a trop peu entrevue dans ses livres.

> Raymond Bellour, *Henri Michaux ou une mesure de l'être*, Gallimard, 1965, p. 235.

Poésie de l'angoisse systématique, elle est haletante, syncopée comme le souffle de l'homme traqué. Poésie de la recherche, qui prétend reconstruire le monde à force de le questionner, elle est un interrogatoire cruel et dense au cours duquel le poète, patient et médecin à la fois, se soumet à une séance d'anamnèse passionnée et interminable. Poésie de la décomposition, elle ne parvient à définir l'indicible, l'innommable que par une contre-création. Poésie de l'harmonie impossible entre l'homme et l'existence, elle se nourrit des analogies discordantes engendrées par de nouveaux rapports entre les mots.

> Melahat Menemencioglu, 'La Recherche de l'expressivité dans la poésie d'Henri Michaux' in *Le Vers français au 20e siècle*, Klincksieck, 1967, p. 220.

C'est bien à une critique de la réalité que Michaux se livre, pour la condamner, la ridiculiser par les moyens les plus divers, allant de l'humour à la cruauté, des fantasmes hallucinatoires qui versent dans la folie onirique aux constats les plus brefs ou condamnations catégoriques. Rien ne résiste à ce bombardement d'analyses poussé par un langage précis, qui défait les bandelettes de l'apparence et du mensonge, pour revenir inlassablement à une primauté de l'imaginaire, le véritable regard de l'homme sur le monde.

> Napoléon Murat, *Michaux*, 'Classiques du XXe siècle', Editions universitaires, 1967, p. 115.

Car tout ce que Michaux nous donne par ses écrits, c'est la chance irremplaçable de changer ce que nous sommes, de nous modifier en vue d'une aventure plus large que celle que nous propose une vie sans écriture, une vie sans électricité, une vie privée de l'immense irruption des signes.

Alain Jouffroy, *La Fin des alternances*, Gallimard, 1970, pp. 205–6.

Laboratoire furieux du hasard et de la mémoire, du plaisir et de la lutte, de la trouvaille et de l'obsession, télescopages de cris et d'éveils, de naissances et de meurtres, agression puis conquête de l'espace, combats d'arrière-garde de l'au-delà, sténographie de l'invisible ou parcours de l'imaginaire, la peinture de Michaux ne cesse de se développer, de s'enrichir, d'accroître ses forces, de s'affirmer, d'intensifier ses rythmes.

Jean-Dominique Rey, 'L'Avenir est au peintre', Catalogue to 1974–5 exhibition of Michaux's works, Galerie Le Point Cardinal, Paris.

NOTES

1. BIOGRAPHY

1. Baudelaire, *Œuvres complètes*, 'Bibliothèque de la Pléiade', Gallimard 1961, pp. 1364–6.

III. THEMES

1. Quoted in M. Nadeau, *Documents surréalistes*, Seuil, 1948, p. 43.
2. Breton, *Manifestes du Surréalisme*, Edns. du Sagittaire, 1946, p. 94.
3. Breton, *Nadja*, Gallimard, 1928, p. 215.
4. Camus, *Le Mythe de Sisyphe* in *Essais*, 'Bibliothèque de la Pléiade', Gallimard, 1965, p. 101.
5. Sartre, *L'Age de raison*, Gallimard, 1945, p. 129.
6. Sartre, *Les Mouches* in *Théâtre*, Gallimard, 1947, p. 102.
7. Camus, *Essais*, p. 101.
8. Sartre, *Théâtre*, p. 61.
9. Camus, *Essais*, p. 128.
10. Rimbaud, *Œuvres* (ed. Bernard), Garnier, 1960, p. 281.
11. Ibid., p. 218.
12. Ibid., p. 346.
13. For more detailed study of the importance of this image, see my edition of *Au Pays de la Magie* (Athlone French Poets, 1977), pp. 21–2, 99–100, 115, 133.
14. Baudelaire, op. cit., p. 1296.
15. For further comments on the theme of the journey, real or imaginary, see my edition of *Au Pays de la Magie*, pp. 1–5.
16. Camus, *Essais*, pp. 107–8.
17. Rimbaud, op. cit., p. 218.
18. Quoted in Nadeau, *Documents surréalistes*, p. 39.
19. Rimbaud, op. cit., p. 345.
20. J.-K. Huysmans, *A Rebours*, Fasquelle, 1903, p. 178.
21. For a full study, see my edition of *Au Pays de la Magie*.
22. See the edition of *Au Pays de la Magie* for the chapter 'The limits of magical creation'.
23. In an interview I had with the poet in 1960.
24. Mallarmé, *Correspondance 1862-1871*, Gallimard, 1959, p. 208.
25. Rimbaud, op. cit., p. 216.
26. Rimbaud, op. cit., p. 345.

27. A. Huxley, *The Doors of Perception* and *Heaven and Hell*, Penguin, 1959, p. 15.

28. Ibid., p. 31.

29. Baudelaire, op. cit., p. 1277.

IV. TECHNIQUES: HUMOUR AND EXORCISM

1. For further comments on the nature of humour in Michaux's work, see my edition of *Au Pays de la Magie*, pp. 40–4.

2. Rimbaud, op. cit., p. 346.

3. J. Cayrol, *Lazare parmi nous*, Seuil, 1950, p. 7.

4. Ibid., p. 16.

V. STYLE AND STRUCTURE

1. Quoted in Mallarmé, *Œuvres complètes*, 'Bibliothèque de la Pléiade', Gallimard, 1945, p. 1489.

VI. POETRY AND PAINTING

1. Cayrol, op. cit., p. 72.

VII. AN EVALUATION

1. Rimbaud, op cit., p. 347.

2. In Alain Jouffroy, *Une Révolution du regard*, Gallimard, 1964, p. 149.

SELECT BIBLIOGRAPHY

For more detailed bibliographical information, especially on Michaux's numerous shorter texts published in limited editions or periodicals and not incorporated into his later collective volumes, readers should consult the following: *Les Cahiers de l'Herne*, No. 8: *Henri Michaux*, 1966, pp. 430–59; G. Place, *Henri Michaux*, Edns. de la Chronique des Lettres françaises, 1969; and M. Bowie, *Henri Michaux*, pp. 195–206.

MICHAUX'S MAJOR WORKS

Qui je fus, Gallimard, 1927.

Ecuador, Gallimard, 1929.

Un Barbare en Asie, Gallimard, 1933.

La Nuit remue, Gallimard, 1935.

Plume précédé de *Lointain intérieur*, Gallimard, 1938.

L'Espace du dedans, pages choisies, Gallimard, 1944.

Epreuves, exorcismes, Gallimard, 1945.

Ailleurs (*Voyage en Grande Garabagne, Au Pays de la Magie, Ici Poddema*), Gallimard, 1948.

La Vie dans les plis, Gallimard, 1949.

Passages, Gallimard, 1950 (revised and expanded edition, 1963).

Face aux verrous, Gallimard, 1954.

Misérable miracle, Edns. du Rocher, 1956 (revised and expanded edition, Gallimard, 1972).

L'Infini turbulent, Mercure de France, 1957.

Connaissance par les gouffres, Gallimard, 1961.

Les grandes épreuves de l'esprit, Gallimard, 1966.

Façons d'endormi, façons d'éveillé, Gallimard, 1969.

Emergences, résurgences, Skira, 1972.

Moments, Gallimard, 1973.

Face à ce qui se dérobe, Gallimard, 1975.

CRITICAL WORKS ON MICHAUX

Badoux, Laurent, *La Pensée de Henri Michaux*, Juris-Verlag, Zurich, 1963.

Béguelin, Marianne, *Henri Michaux, esclave et démiurge*, L'Age d'Homme, Lausanne, 1973.

Bellour, Raymond, *Henri Michaux ou une mesure de l'être*, 'Les Essais', Gallimard, 1965.

Bertelé, René, *Henri Michaux*, 'Poètes d'aujourd'hui', Seghers, 1946 (revised editions 1957, 1965).

Bowie, Malcolm, *Henri Michaux, a study of his literary works*, Oxford University Press, 1973.

Bréchon, Robert, *Michaux*, 'Bibliothèque idéale', Gallimard, 1959 (revised edition 1969).

Cahiers de l'Herne, No. 8, 1966: special number devoted to Michaux.

Coulon, Philippe de, *Henri Michaux, poète de notre société*, Edns. de la Baconnière, Neuchâtel, 1949.

Dadoun, Roger, *Ruptures sur Henri Michaux*, Payot, 1976.

Gide, André, *Découvrons Henri Michaux*, Gallimard, 1941.

Jouffroy, Alain, *Henri Michaux*, 'Musée de poche', Edns. Georges Fall, 1961.

Loras, Olivier, *Rencontre avec Henri Michaux au plus profond des gouffres*, J. and S. Bleyon, 1967.

Murat, Napoléon, *Henri Michaux*, 'Classiques du XXe siècle', Edns. universitaires, 1967.

Promesse, Nos. 19–20, 1967: special number devoted to Michaux.

INDEX

Athlone French Poets

General Editor EILEEN LE BRETON
Reader in French Language and Literature,
Bedford College, University of London

Monographs

GERARD DE NERVAL
THEOPHILE GAUTIER
VERLAINE
JULES LAFORGUE
GUILLAUME APOLLINAIRE
SAINT-JOHN PERSE
HENRI MICHAUX

Critical Editions

VICTOR HUGO : CHATIMENTS
GERARD DE NERVAL : LES CHIMERES
ALFRED DE MUSSET : CONTES D'ESPAGNE ET D'ITALIE
THEOPHILE GAUTIER : POESIES
PAUL VERLAINE : SAGESSE
PAUL VERLAINE : ROMANCES SANS PAROLES
ARTHUR RIMBAUD : LES ILLUMINATIONS
JULES LAFORGUE : LES COMPLAINTES
PAUL VALERY : CHARMES OU POEMES
GUILLAUME APOLLINAIRE : ALCOOLS
SAINT-JOHN PERSE : EXIL
MICHAUX : AU PAYS DE LA MAGIE